THE SWINDLER is not, as a rule, a thug. He will not blackmail. He will not murder. Your daughter is reasonably safe with him. He never carries a gun, only some misleading visiting cards, some forged letters and perhaps an extra passport or two and, frequently, a curious pack of cards. With these complicated but harmless bits of paper he sets out to rob you painlessly, until the last distressing extraction.

The Great Swindlers, Judge Gerald Sparrow.

CONNED

SCAMS, FRAUDS AND SWINDLES

James Morton and Hilary Bateson

Illustrated by Chris Duggan

PORTRAIT

Visit the Portrait website!

Portrait publishes a wide range of non-fiction, including biography, history, science, music, popular culture and sport.

If you want to:
- read descriptions of our popular titles
- buy our books over the Internet
- take advantage of our special offers
- enter our monthly competition
- learn more about your favourite Portrait authors

VISIT OUR WEBSITE AT: www.portraitbooks.co.uk

For Jeremy Beadle, J.P. Bean, Jim and Sherry Ratcliffe

Acknowledgements

Our thanks are due to Jeremy Beadle; J. P. Bean; Alan Brooke; Denise Dwyer; Francine Levitov; Barbara Levy; Jim and Sherry Ratcliffe as well as the staff at the British Library; the Newspaper Library, Colindale; the National Archives, Kew; the Mitchell Library, Sydney; the New York Public Library; the State Library of Victoria, Melbourne; the State Library of Western Australia, Perth and the State Library of Queensland, Brisbane.

Contents

How to be a good conman

IN THE 1930s the great conman 'Count' Victor Lustig (*see* page 2) set out the basic rules for the successful confidence trickster. Most are still relevant today:

- Be a good listener.

- Never give a political opinion until the mark (potential victim) has expressed his and then agree.

- Wait for the mark to reveal his religion, and then become a member of the same church.

- Hint at sex, but don't pursue it unless the mark is eager to explore the subject.

- Never discuss personal ailments unless the mark has shown an interest in the subject.

- Never be untidy or drunk, yet always be ready for a party.

- Never appear bored.

- Never probe, let the mark volunteer information.

- Never brag, let the mark sense your success.

'Count' Victor Lustig

PERHAPS THE greatest of all conmen has been 'Count' Victor Lustig, born in Prague in 1890, who 'ennobled' himself after serving short prison sentences for false pretences in Austria and Switzerland before the First World War.

It was, however, in Paris in 1925 working with his partner 'Dapper' Dan Collins that Lustig came into his own when he twice sold the Eiffel Tower for scrap. When the scam was finally discovered, the Count hurriedly left Europe for the US, where for the next two decades he lived principally off the Money Box – a false money-making scam. Apparently Lustig never received less than US$4,000 for his machine, which cost $15 to make. Two pool-room owners in Montana paid $43,000 for one of them, a businessman in Kansas City paid $25,000 and the top dollar was $100,000 from a Californian.

It is said that he also once swindled Al Capone out of $50,000 but repaid the money rather than face the great man's wrath. Capone, so the story goes – although it does not appear in any of the major Capone biographies – was so impressed with his honesty that he gave the Count $5,000 dollars to help him on his way. Other versions have it that Lustig never intended to do anything but give Capone his money back to impress him with his honesty.

Unfortunately for Lustig, he abandoned the Money Box and took to straightforward counterfeiting. During a five-year period in the early 1930s he is said to have disposed of over $2.3 million in fake money. It is a mark of his ability that he persuaded a Texas sheriff, Q.R. Miller, to invest in a scheme and later talked him into stealing $65,000 from county funds to make a further investment. Even more remarkable is that Miller went to jail without giving Lustig up to save himself.

Lustig's great ability was to change tack at a crucial moment. In most con tricks there is a moment when the mark's appetite is whetted by a glimpse of the rich rewards just beyond the horizon.

Lustig was quite capable of what was called a 'reverser', explaining just how dangerous it would be for the mark to invest money. He worked this scam with Estelle Sweeny, who had been Miss Peoria and runner-up for Miss Illinois and had gone to Hollywood where she had a bit part in a film under the name Stellar Swan.

In 1926 he persuaded a farm-machinery manufacturer, Ronald Dodge, to invest $34,000 in a new Broadway production, which was going to feature this talentless child. When Dodge became interested in the venture Ludwig began to point out the dangers; for example, that a few bad reviews would force the show to close. All that happened was that Dodge became more and more interested in his role of impresario. Lustig was to put up $32,000 so that Dodge would be the senior partner.

When Dodge arrived at Lustig's hotel with the money they went to a bar to celebrate. After a few minutes Lustig was called to the telephone and Dodge was left in the bar. When it dawned on him that Lustig was not coming back, he went in search of Swan whom he believed was an accomplice. Some time later he found her working in burlesque and, the story goes, on learning she had also been tricked by Lustig, he gave the girl $200 to go home to Peoria.

The Count was finally caught in May 1935 in Manhattan after a tip-off when stacks of money, along with counterfeit plates, were found in a locker at a railway station. He was remanded, pending his finding a $50,000 bond, to the Federal House of Detention in West Street from where, shortly before 1.00 p.m. on 25 August, a man wearing dungarees was seen cleaning a window on the third floor of the building. He appeared to drop the rag he was using but, rather like a conjurer's ribbon, it lengthened into sheets and the Count descended it rapidly. Some of the onlookers say he fell at the end, but in any event he was able to pick himself up and trot off over the cobblestones into the waterfront traffic. It was not the Count's first escape. As Albert Grauman he had sawn his way out of Lake County jail in Crown Point, Indiana.

Lustig did not last long on the outside. He was recognised and recaptured in Pittsburgh within the month. On his return to New York, he treated his admirers to an account of the details of his escape. Sent to Alcatraz, where he was known as 'King Con', to serve a 20-year sentence, he was later transferred to Leavenworth where he died in 1947.

The old cons are the best

THE OLD SCAMS still remain the best. On 17 June 1996 David Billson and David Rice were each jailed for 21 months at Southwark Crown Court for what, strictly incorrectly, was described as a Green Goods Swindle. They had produced a machine capable of making $100 bills and, after successfully selling a number in the US, had come to England to promote it. In fact this was the Money Box Swindle rather than the Green Goods trick.

The Money Box probably originated in ancient Egypt but it was first patented as a toy in 1891 in Vienna. Very soon afterwards it was in the hands of the professionals. Over the years there have, of course, been variations and improvements but, basically, a small box is shown to potential clients. A genuine note is placed on top of a stack of paper cut into banknote size. The victim is told that special plates have been installed and paper obtained from a source in the Treasury. The machine's handle is then turned and, to the delight of the mark, out spew apparently newly printed notes. In fact they are bank-notes which have been planted in the box's false bottom. To heighten the tension, by keeping the mark thinking about the money, the operator can leave the 'notes' in the machine overnight for them to be impregnated with ink and to dry out. Once the demonstration is concluded the mark parts with his money for the machine rather than for the notes.

THE GREEN Goods Swindle itself dates back to the end of the American Civil War but it is only a version of the older Sawdust Game worked in Britain. Basically punters are shown genuine notes which they are told are fake. They are then offered the chance to buy a quantity at a discount. At the last minute these are switched and the mark ends up with cut green paper. In one 1882 brochure advertising Green Goods the going rate for these bills was $600 for $10,000 worth.

A variation is that sometimes investors do get to see a suitcase full of what appears to be their money. They are not, however, allowed to take it with them and will be told that they may have it the next day after it has been dyed black to hide it from the enquiring eyes of customs officials. Sometimes they will have to make an additional payment to buy the stain remover. It is even possible they may get to take away the suitcase, now full of dyed and cut newspaper.

In 2006 two businessmen in Malaysia paid $14,000 for a suitcase of US dollars. The notes were painted black and the dupes were told that this was to enable them to smuggle the notes out of the country. They were shown how the notes could be cleaned and were sent on their way only to be arrested at the border.

WORKING IN Denver, in the mid-1880s, was Jefferson Randolph Smith. He was born in Newnan, Georgia, and known as 'Soapy' because his stock in trade was selling bars of soap with the possibility of bills worth up to $100 under the wrappers. Shills (accomplices) in the crowd would rip off a wrapper and shout that they had won a prize, but they were the only ones to do so. He also opened the gambling hell the Tivoli Club, which had a sign, 'Caveat Emptor', over the entrance. From there he ran crooked dice and poker games while his brother, Bascomb, ran 'sure thing' stock exchanges and fake diamond auctions.

With the anti-gambling reforms in Denver in the early 1890s he moved to run a similar operation in Credde, Colorado, and after returning for a spell in Denver he went to Skagway, Alaska, during the 1897 gold rush. With the start of the Spanish–American war the following year, he elected himself Captain of the Skagway Military Company, a volunteer army that he used to control the town for his own ends.

On 7 July 1898 John Stewart, a Klondike miner, lost a sack of gold to three of Smith's gang in a Three Card Monte Game. He refused to pay and the gold was snatched from him. The next night, local vigilantes held a meeting on the town's wharf, to deal with undesirables such as Soapy. Fighting broke out and Smith and a guard, Frank Reid, exchanged fire. Soapy Smith died immediately and Reid 12 days after.

THE GREAT THING about the Gold Brick Swindle is that in one of its forms it appeals to all. Bricks were sold to people who were trying to protect their fortunes at a time when hoarding gold was illegal. In other cases, the buyers think they are benefitting from the fact that the gold is stolen, because they are getting it cheap. They might be – if they weren't buying gold-coated lead or brass.

The swindle seems to have originated in the Californian gold-fields of the 1850s. The original story was that of a miner who had discovered a fabulous motherlode but had to sell a brick almost at cost because he was strapped for cash. The scam spread across the West like a prairie fire; the none too wholesome sheriff Wyatt Earp, who along with his partner Dave Mather worked the scam in Mobetie, Texas, was one of the early tricksters. In this case cowboys were persuaded they were buying part of a shipment of stolen Mexican gold.

The trick, in its improved form, was brought to New York by former Illinois college boy Reed Waddell in 1880 when he sold his first brick for $4,000. Before Reed there had been plenty of painted bricks with a plug of gold inserted in them. But now, along with his usual patter that he needed the money to return west and mine the lode, he would take the sucker to what seemed to be a US assayer's office where an accomplice valued it at a minimum of $10,000. If the marks proved recalcitrant he would dig out the plug and give it to them to be examined by their own jeweller. No, he couldn't part with the whole brick because he had to show it to other prospective purchasers.

Waddell is said to have made $250,000 before moving into the Green Goods Swindle in which he and Tom O'Brien took $500,000 from suckers at Chicago's World's Fair in 1893. The previous year O'Brien, regarded by New York police chief Thomas Byrnes as the 'King of Bunco Men' – or fraudsters – had been given a ten-year term for swindling a farmer in Albany, New York out of $10,000. He escaped a month into his sentence and went to Europe.

In March 1895 the pair quarrelled over the division of profits and O'Brien shot Waddell at the Gare du Nord in Paris. Waddell, an early seller of the Brooklyn Bridge, died on 3 April and his body was shipped home to Springfield, Illinois where it is buried near to that of Abraham Lincoln. In March 1896 O'Brien was put on trial in Paris, and told the court Waddell had hit him earlier in the evening at the Café Americaine. In fact, said his counsel, the shooting was almost self-defence. He was sentenced to life imprisonment.

ANOTHER VERSION of the Gold Brick Swindle was run in the 1890s by Jacob Sondheim, who worked as Al Wise or Wilson. He persuaded men he was the owner of a process by which genuine gold coins could be sweated, or reduced in weight, without damage to their appearance. Clients were persuaded to install tanks in the basements of their homes and put in 10,000 or 20,000 gold coins for treatment in Sondheim's special solution. The tanks were iron vats with locked covers. The speculators held keys but, unfortunately for them, so did Sondheim.

A SCAM BASED on the Gold Brick Swindle is being worked today in Hong Kong. Two women approach another woman, often elderly, in the street saying they work on a building site and show her a genuine gold ring, which they say they have dug up. There are plenty more where that came from but they are illegal immigrants and so do not have the necessary identification papers to sell them themselves. Will she buy them? The remaining rings are, of course, fakes.

ANOTHER OLD short con was the professional fit-thrower, such as Edward Gray who would throw himself on the pavement, writhing, and hope that passers-by, or the owner of the house in front of which he put on his act, would give him money to go to hospital or for food. He served nine months in New York in 1902 after he had faked a heart attack in front of a policeman who recognised him from his description.

ONE OF THE easiest short cons to work is the Corner Game, sometimes known, because of the alleged simplicity of the Irish, as the Murphy or Paddy Game. Practised in red-light districts, the victim is the punter who is looking for illicit entertainment such as a blue film or an assignment with a near-beer hostess (girls who worked at premises which pretended to, but didn't, sell alcohol). He pays his money and is told to go round the corner where, in five or ten minutes' time, the man with the projector or the girl will appear; in fact, neither do so. In the case of the girl the punter has met in Soho, he is usually sent further afield, to outside the Ritz hotel or by Big Ben. When the police officer Nipper Read, who later arrested the Krays, was trying to clean up the West End prior to the 1966 World Cup he came across one Dutch seaman who had paid £100 and been sent to Morden, at the very end of the Northern Line.

In the heyday of the blue-film racket, the tout would stand outside an open doorway spieling to the punters and possibly showing them postcards which he claimed showed explicit sex scenes from the film. Sometimes he would accompany them to the room and ask them to wait while he went to check the projector. At the very best they would see a film of a woman undressing or nudists playing volleyball.

A modern version surfaced in Austria in late 2006 when a bogus priest and his girlfriend persuaded a pensioner in Linz that he could have a bath with the naked girl on payment of the equivalent of £100. They ran the bath for him, he undressed and got in. After waiting ten minutes he heard cupboard doors being opened and when the girl did not appear, he got out of the bath to find they had taken his cash.

THE NOW ALMOST extinct con game of Banco is a version of the old English game Eight Dice Cloth. Although, on the face of it, it is simple, honest and foolproof, it is not. There are 28 spaces on a cloth which pay prizes; 13 also have stars which do not; one is blank. A number of dice are rolled or small denomination cards drawn. If the victim draws a star number he must pay to throw again. The trick is when, after he has been allowed to win a small amount, he draws number 27 which is a conditional prize. The condition is that he puts in whatever sum of money the trickster thinks he can stand. Unfortunately once the money is in place he will inevitably draw the blank and lose all.

Oscar Wilde is said to have lost thousands to 'Hungry Joe' Lewis playing Banco in his tours of the mining camps, but it is more likely that he lost the money in New York where they were both staying in the Hotel Brunswick. Wilde stopped the cheque. On 27 May 1885 Lewis received four years after he relieved an Englishman Joseph Ramsden of £250 in a version of the Three Card Trick. Inspector Byrnes of the New York Police thought Lewis had 'victimised more people by the Banco Game than any other five men in the profession'.

Seventy years later, Banco reappeared in a slightly different form as the Indian Rug Game. Shortly after the Second World War when tourism was on the increase in Nevada, cars were not as reliable as they are today, roads were poor and there was no such thing as air-conditioning in the ordinary owner's car. It was desirable, if not essential, to make regular stops. This allowed both the engine to cool down and the driver and passengers to stretch their legs. So, throughout the state, a series of tourist attractions in the form of small zoos or snake shows developed. Some were good, with the owners actually knowledgeable about the snakes. Others merely had an ageing and ailing racoon on show and when out-of-state tourists pulled up, a man who had seemingly stopped at the same time would often casually walk up to meet them. A friendly remark would be passed as they went into the show and throughout the tour the stranger would make small talk with both the tourists and the show promoter, discussing the animals on display. The show would usually end in what amounted to a maze, with the tourists going along with the stranger and of course the promoter, into a small room. There the stranger would apparently notice an Indian blanket and would turn the conversation to gambling by Indians.

The promoter would admit that there was some gambling by Indians, and, when pressed, would agree to show the tourists how it worked. Indians were, he would say, very conservative gamblers; indeed the Indian Rug Game was one where it was almost impossible to lose. Under more pressure he would reluctantly give a demonstration. With nine or 11 dice the losing number was 26, which was almost impossible to throw. The player had to throw the same number as on the first roll before he threw a 26. It was, of course, a highly dangerous form of craps where seven is the losing number. All other numbers were stand-offs requiring another roll of the dice. Would the tourist like a go at this cast-iron way of making money? You bet. One dollar was put up by the house and one by the tourist.

Unsurprisingly it was a stand-off. It is difficult enough to add the numbers on two dice, let alone 11, before they are swept away.

Now came the problem for the mark. It was double-your-money time; and again and again and again until in some cases the mark had been cleaned out of all travelling money. After all, if you know you cannot lose in the end you are reluctant to let your potential winnings disappear because you can't raise your stake for the next throw. Worse, in front of other people you don't want to admit you cannot. The house was very fair. If a punter ran out of money the stakes were not forfeit. It was simply a question of finding a player or players who would club together and put in the next stake. Sometimes the game would be suspended while the punter was 'put on the send' and went home or to a bank to draw more money.

The difficulty was that matters did not stop there. Some punters realised they had been taken in a scam and the bolder – and possibly more foolhardy – decided to do something about it. First, they had to cross a desert to find a sheriff's office or outpost of the gaming commission and often they were followed and threatened, literally at the doors of the office. Sometimes their cars were snatched.

THE THREE CARD Trick, known as Three Card Monte in the US where it has been running for centuries, is just that – a trick on the mugs who try to find the Queen as opposed to one of two Aces. It should not be possible, but if by a hideous accident it is, then the dealers and his team take steps to ensure there is no payout. The punter, who will have watched a number of people apparently winning, is shown the Queen and the Aces which are then shuffled and placed face down on the board – alternatively, the cards are moved while face down. The dealer's spiel is more or less standard: 'Men, I have here three little cards, two red Aces and the black Queen of Spades. The idea is for you to find the Queen. If you find it you win;

if you turn up an Ace you lose. It's as simple as that. And remember, I take no bets from paupers, cripples, or pregnant women. I show you all three cards, then throw them face down – fast like this. If your eye is faster than my hand and you find the Queen, I pay you the same amount you bet. Remember men, if you don't speculate you can't accumulate. Money in hand or no bet ...'

The dealer will seemingly have signalled to the punter which card is the Queen – the corner is sometimes bent – but when he has placed his bet the mug will be amazed to find he has chosen wrongly and an Ace also has a bent corner. If he has accidentally got it right then shills in the crowd will claim that it is their bet and there will be a redeal, which the punter will certainly lose. In extremis, a lookout, known in Australia as a cockatoo, will call out that the police are coming and the team will vanish, leaving the punter with the cards, or nothing at all. There can be up to four or five shills in any game. When the three-card tricksters appeared at the central London courts the magistrates would refuse them time to pay the fines: 'Yours is a cash business, and so is mine.'

Amazingly, in 1912 the Divisional Court held the Three Card Trick to be a game of skill, which of course it was – by the operator. Two years later it was held that when there was cheating during play this was an offence under the Gaming Act 1845.

THE VERY similar Shell Game, in which the mug punter has to find under which of three shells a pea is hidden, probably dates back to ancient Egypt and has certainly been played for centuries. Again the punter cannot win. The trick is done by sleight of hand and there is no pea under any shell until after the mug has chosen wrongly. The dealer produces the pea under what would have been the winning shell – had it been there in the first place.

STILL ON THE street, one of the standard cons is when someone bumps into you and drops a pair of previously broken spectacles or a mobile telephone, and so on. You are then expected to pay for the damage. In certain districts in Tokyo in the 1960s, pedestrians would bump into a car and while they were writhing on the ground a hostile crowd gathered blaming the driver for their supposed injuries. The scam is now particularly popular in African countries.

THE GYPSY Blessing Game has been worked for centuries and, almost unbelievably, is still in use. Basically the victim is told that he, his family and particularly his money are under an evil spell and the only thing that can be done is to buy one's way out. Naturally the money to be paid to remove the evil spell has to be handed over to the conman who acts as an intervener. Sometimes, the money paid by the mark would be sewn in a cloth and buried in a churchyard. When the trick was worked in New York sometimes a handkerchief was thrown from the Staten Island ferry. In neither case was the money actually in the cloth when it was buried, or in the hand-kerchief when it hit the water.

Other versions from the days when gypsies travelled from house to house selling lucky heather included holding a punter's wallet to bless his money, telling him that $100 would multiply eightfold within the month. By sleight of hand the money was out of the wallet before it was returned. Another variation was for the money to be flushed down the lavatory by the owner. In this case the pipes had been tampered with: the conman had stuffed them so that the money wasn't flushed into the sewer and could be retrieved later.

IN THE PAST year a new version of the Gypsy Blessing Game has been operated by fake police officers in Prague. Tourists are stopped and asked to produce their wallets for inspection for forged currency. The money is then palmed and replaced with out-of-date Bulgarian notes. Another version is that the 'policemen' who arrive on the scene simply confiscate the money or disappear into the crowd while the victim is distracted.

The Gypsy Blessing Game is also still being worked in South America, and in March 2006 in Argentina a blessing took place which resulted in the loss of an iPod as well as money. The victim was given a houseplant by a man in the street and told to put it next to her wallet so that he could bless the money in it to ensure her safe travel. He pickpocketed her while she was holding the plant.

Another variation is for the first member of a team to spray tomato ketchup or juice over the back of the victim. He will then point this out to the victim, and, as he is helping to clean up the mess other members of the team will steal the victim's possessions. In recent years this has been particularly popular in Barcelona.

ONE OF THE many talented Australian conmen of the 1920s was the Sydney-born William Donaldson known as 'Bill the Boatman', then in his sixties. He was first convicted as William Mitchell on 27 March 1896 when he received three months for false pretences.

In 1922 he was arrested near Russell Square in Central London along with an equally talented South African running the then very popular Will Fraud. He had a copy of the *Evening News* of 19 January with what purported to be an item in the STOP PRESS:

£60,000 FOR CHARITY

The celebrated will case of O'Connor v. O'Connor was concluded today.

A lucky Irishman inherits £300,000 of which £60,000 has to be distributed by gentlemen of independent means knowing personally the needs and wants of the people receiving the money the distributor receiving 10 per cent without incurring any responsibility, strange to say all charitable organisations and religious societies are excluded from participation. His Lordship also commended the highly practical idea of personal distribution by respectable gentlemen.

The con was a simple one. A suitable looking punter was persuaded that he was the ideal person to be part of the distribution process. At the very worst he would receive £6,000 and the criminally inclined might actually keep the whole haul. Naturally he had to put up security to be part of the team and in return he would get a briefcase full of newspaper.

There were a number of teams working the scam in London at the time. Earlier that year Donaldson had been put on an identification parade for a £900 swindle in Hampstead and had not been picked out. Two others were later arrested.

It may seem amazing but the scam was still in operation long after the Second World War. It died out when the evening papers no longer printed a STOP PRESS.

A VARIATION OF the scam is still alive and well, if being played for bigger stakes. In 1999 an attempt was made to swindle officials of St Paul's Cathedral out of £100 million. Posing as devout worshippers and film producers the story was that in return for a short-term immediate investment of £100 million, the swindlers would donate £50 million, which would pay for the restoration of the dome. In June 2002 an Italian male model, who was charged with the offence, received a six-month sentence. Two other suspects had skipped bail and the Crown dropped proceedings against a fourth man. Members of the gang had already failed in a similar attempt to take money from Marlborough School.

ONE OF THE longest-running door-to-door scams has been that of the Williamson clan, who arrived in the US in the 1890s. Of Scottish origin, they have a loose-knit operation said to be in the region of 5,000 strong working out of Pennsylvania. They first came to light as a group around 1938 and they have been operating since then throughout the US. Seeking better weather, the family has been targeting Southern California for some years where their children are placed in public schools for the duration of the swindle

Basically the extended family descends like locusts on an area, where the con is to do a good repair job on a house in a neighbourhood and then tour adjoining streets saying they have materials left over to do just one more house. Now, fake lightening rods are sold and asphalt, thinned by crank-case oil, is put down. They leave before the poor weather comes and the paint starts to run and the asphalt is washed away in the rain. Then it is off to base camp in the mid-West until the next year.

IN THE GREAT days of the transatlantic liners, some of the conmen on board would be cardsharps or what were then known as 'Deep Sea Divers'. The mug punter would be allowed to win until the one last big game just before the ship docked. One of the more talented players was Julius 'Nicky' Arnstein, husband of singer Fanny Brice and a friend and confederate of the gambler Arnold Rothstein. When, in the 1920s, New York's Assistant Chief Inspector John L. Sullivan commented to one of Arnstein's potential victims that he should surely know he was about to be fleeced, he received the reply, 'Of course I know, but he's better company than the honest men on board this ship.'

ONE OF THE simplest and most rewarding of cons seems to have originated with the assassination of President James A. Garfield in 1881. After his death suitably worded advertisements appeared coast to coast offering a rare portrait of the former president. The cost was a dollar – and in return the punter received a 5-cent postage stamp. Flushed with success the operators extended the scheme to Abraham Lincoln 'done from a photograph by Mathew Brady' and, in England, Queen Victoria. From time to time, to keep costs down, used stamps were sent to purchasers.

Over the years there have been other postal frauds offering punters such treats as a guaranteed way to 'Double your money' – which was simply to 'Fold it in half' – and another guaranteed way to get rid of moths – 'Soak the item in kerosene and set it alight'.

ONE BIRMINGHAM conman of the 1880s was John Hartwell who, as 'The Great English Seer', forecast the possibility of marriage for the gullible – price six stamps. When some newspapers refused to take his advertisements he changed sex, becoming 'Anna Ross, the Great American Seer'. Of course soothsayers were not exclusively English. There were plenty in the US of whom Professor Castrala, 'The Great Spanish Seer', was one. He had an almost identical line in patter: 'Send me your age, a lock of hair, the colour of your eyes, 25 cents and a 3-cent stamp and I will provide a correct picture of your future husband or wife, the place and time of the first meeting and the date of your marriage.' The Professor turned out to be a man named Harris who had run *demi-mondaine* balls in Memphis but, being temporarily out of funds, had taken up soothsaying.

THE SIMPLE version of the Badger Game, known in Australia as the Ginger Game and which has been worked over the centuries all over the world, involves a woman taking a man to her room. When he is almost completely undressed and she is partly clothed, in bursts her husband/uncle/father/brother/probation officer, and so on. The role played will depend upon the apparent age of the girl. Money is then extorted from the man to assuage the family's feelings or, if the girl is seemingly young, to pay for a period in a hospital to allow her to recover from her terrible experience.

THE END OF the American Civil War saw a new development in the art of the conman. Until then most cons had been 'the short con'. That did not mean to say that a conman or woman would not adopt and maintain an identity for some years, but essentially they worked alone or in a small team and the gulls could be described as the victims of in-and-out raids. Now came a completely new scam: the Big Store, a major confidence game operation.

The Big Store was what appeared to be a stockbrokers' office or betting shop, where tourists were conned into putting up cash for investment on dud stock or fixed horse races. Every single person in the room, reading the financial or sporting papers, drinking tea, making bets, or sweeping up, was part of the team in place to con the marks into believing they were in a real office, poolroom, and so on. It came into its own in the late 1890s with a number of operators – including New York's Joseph 'Paper Joe' Bessimer, or Kratalsky, who is said to have died a millionaire – making a fortune from the scam.

Once Soapy Smith left Denver, the French Canadian Lou Blonger 'The Fixer', who more or less ran crime in the town for nearly 40 years from the end of the nineteenth century, ran a long series of Big Stores. But the greatest exponents were the New York-based Gondorff brothers, Fred and Charley, who operated from the end of the century until 1915. They were reputed to have taken a St Louis pawnbroker for $200,000 in 1899 and each year they found up to 20 victims for what appeared to be a bookmaking parlour in Manhattan.

The betting scam was simple and relied on the greed and dishonesty of the punter, who was told that an ex-employee of the telegraph office, often a 'relative' who had been sacked, could key into the wires and obtain racing results before they were known to the betting office. These he would pass to the fixer who would induce the mark to have a very substantial bet as he himself did. When the bet lost, the fixer would apparently be just as upset as the mark who would put the whole thing down to experience.

It all went wrong for Charley Gondorf in 1914 when an English-man, Eugene Adams, was the victim of a variation of the scam. This time he was allowed to win at offices on West 49th Street. He had put up a cheque to bet on the long-hot winner but was told that he would have to put down cash against his winnings before he could collect. He returned with the money and when he showed the $4,600 to two of Gondorf's men he was handed a sealed bag, which apparently contained his winnings. At that moment, in burst 'policemen'. Adams's wallet was snatched but, instead of running away as he was expected to do, he ran after the thieves. Later Gondorf made an arrangement with Adams to return his wallet if he dropped charges of deception and went to Canada, but the handover at the corner of 59th street and Broadway was watched and Gondorf was arrested. Despite numerous previous arrests he had never been put on trial and faced a jury before. But this time a guilty verdict was returned in ten minutes and he received five to ten years in Sing Sing. The next year his brother Fred followed him down. The last scene in the film *The Sting* is based on their Manhattan operation. Another Big Store, this time a broker's office, appears in *The Grifters*.

The Big Store is still being worked today. High-class fraudsters will be quite happy to meet their victims in top-class hotels or restaurants. Rooms may be booked in buildings where well-known banks and other financial institutions have offices. Other investors who attend the meeting may well be stooges.

THE LONG FIRM Fraud or LF is really only a variation of the Big Store; but, in this con, the financial mark never gets to see the operator. In its simplest form a business in, say, ladies' dresses is set up, goods are bought on credit and paid for. The operation is then expanded to include perhaps household goods or children's toys. More goods are bought and then, when a line of credit has been established, a very substantial amount of goods are bought, sold off below cost, the premises closed and the bank is out of its money.

In slightly more sophisticated versions, such as those that were run on behalf of the Kray Twins by their financial adviser Leslie Payne, cells of LFs were set up, each providing cross-references for the others. The dangers to the promoters were few: if possible, goods were ordered over the telephone; staff were employed on a casual basis for a very short time so ensuring a rapid turnover of employees, which led to problems determining who ordered the goods if any questions were asked. Managers would usually be associates with no previous criminal record. If there was a prosecution the failure of the business could be put down to poor trading conditions and general mismanagement rather than fraud. In these circumstances, during the 1950s and 1960s, in Britain when the LFs were at their peak the chances of conviction were slight.

Princess Soltykoff

ONE OF THE MOST engaging conwomen at the beginning of the last century was the Princess Soltykoff or, rather more prosaically, Margaret Trew Prebble, who received two sentences for fraud in the early 1900s. When she appeared at the Central Criminal Court charged with a variety of offences of obtaining goods by false pretences, at least one journalist was entranced by her appearance. On 6 February 1906 she was described by the *Morning Leader*, as 'entertainingly beautiful' when it was alleged that, as Lady Muriel Paget, she had been defrauding shops and stores in the West End. The writer for the *Leader* was clearly half in love with her:

> ... rich complexion, medium height, commanding presence, mass of beautiful brown hair, elegantly dressed and full of Southern fire, her mouth is the work of an actress and her manner – even in moments of excitement – is quite the manner of the old nobility.

Unfortunately, George Elliott, for the prosecution, claimed that she was no more the Princess, let alone Lady Muriel, than he was a Mohammedan. She was, he said, born on 1 December 1873, the fifth daughter of a joiner James McKillem who lived at Upper Mason Street, Liverpool.

She had first struck, obtaining a miniature painting from Esme Collings of Bond Street, by pretending her cousin was the Marquess of Anglesey. She had then conducted operations with addresses, such as the fine-sounding Winwick Hall, Haydock (a lunatic asylum), Portslade (where she had been a probationary nurse), Arundel Square (a boarding house in Barnsbury) and that well-known retreat for swindlers of the day, the Metropole Hotel in Brighton. It was alleged that the hat she was so fashionably wearing in court had also been obtained by fraud.

Her trial was clearly an entertaining one. The genuine Lady Muriel Paget, wearing furs, although the court was suffocatingly hot, gave evidence that she was the one and only Lady P. and she had never met the Princess.

Then after a sister had given evidence of the Princess's lowly birth, into the witness box went the lady herself. She 'looked a tragedy Queen in a long red "wrapper" reaching from neck to feet and produced a large family Bible which she kissed'.

Asked her name, she replied Nina Olga Trew-Prebble. Asked where she was born, Judge Rentoul interrupted, 'Surely that is hearsay' – [laughter from the court]. She said she had been educated at Liverpool College and Windsor College at the expense of Major Paget (the Hon. Alfred).

It was at this point in her evidence that the usher decided that, unlike Elliott, she was indeed a Mohammedan and therefore had taken the oath incorrectly. Now she had to take off her boots and slippers, place one hand on the Koran and one on her forehead. Would she mind taking off her boots?

'We'll look the other way,' said Elliot.

'I don't mind,' replied the Princess. But, reported the *Leader*, no one did look the other way.

Once correctly sworn, she said she had changed her name in 1892 to Slolterfoht. Who was he? A boy who had made lucky investments for her. She had changed her name to Paget two years later when she was stranded in Paris. In her earlier days she had wanted to study medicine and had once run a bakery in Everton before she went on the stage, which she left to marry Prince Alexis Soltykoff. They had tried to marry in Scotland but, when she discovered they had not stayed the requisite period, they married again in St Petersburg. Unfortunately she had given the marriage papers to a woman she had met in a convent and had never seen them again. She had left the Prince in St Petersburg and had returned to England 'under the guardianship of an old gentleman'.

When she learned that Alexis had died in a Russian prison, using the name Slolterfoht she had married a man named Prebble who had been 'at the Varsity' and had been studying medicine at Guy's Hospital until funds ran out and he joined the army. It was never clear whether he had joined up simply to escape the Princess.

Summing up, Judge Rentoul, acting on the belief that the working classes cannot have intelligent children, was clearly captivated with her as well: 'A person of undoubted ability, particularly so when it is considered that she is the daughter of a joiner.' The jury took half an hour to find her guilty.

It was then that the Princess's nemesis, Inspector Drew, told the court about her. She had left home in 1893 after her mother had made 'an accusation'. Mother was right because the Princess-to-be had given birth to Annette Tarbett McKillem on 10 April 1894 in Liverpool. She then became a children's nurse in Wales and was apparently well thought of and out of trouble before a kindly clergyman did his Christian duty and travelled to Wales to denounce her to the family she was working for. On her credit side she had saved a child trapped in a fire in an upstairs tenement room.

What, the judge wanted to know, was the truth of the marriage? Soltykoff's father had denied any union. 'Could it have been a secret marriage?' asked the judge and anyway where was Soltykoff *fils*? Definitely dead. So that mystery was never explained.

Any previous? Fifteen months at Suffolk Assizes for fraud in August 1902 in not very dissimilar circumstances. She had been dismissed from a nursing position for obtaining goods on credit and was in Johannesburg for a period of time. Some of her bills were paid by a peer, but unpaid ones included £47 at the Savoy and one bill at the Hotel Cecil, where she had left a worthless packet which she had said contained jewels. In 1901 she was working at a nurses' home in Ipswich where a lady befriended her and took her to Southwold. There she was the widow of Prince Alexis, and the unfortunate Prebble had, without his knowledge, been commissioned and was now a major. The prosecution thought that Prebble was in fact a corporal. That escapade ended when she went to London and ran up another hotel bill. She was obliged to leave in a hurry because her brother had been badly injured in a shooting accident in Southwold. She had also tried to obtain money from a Liverpool shipowner, pretending she was his daughter. In fact Prince Soltykoff, a member of the Jockey Club, had earlier given evidence at the Suffolk Assizes and admitted it was possible his son had married the adventuress.

Rentoul thought it was worth five years, but instead he sentenced her to 18 months with hard labour remarking, 'She will probably be doing the same thing over again.' But there does not seem to be any further record of her misdemeanours.

Room at the top

ONE OF THE abiding legends of the Terror of the French Revolution was that somehow Louis-Charles de France – second son of Louis XVI and Marie Antoinette – who became Dauphin on the death of his brother in 1789 and was thought to have died at the age of 10 in 1795 of a scrofulous infection while imprisoned in the Temple, had instead been smuggled out and was alive and well and living under a variety of guises. After the final defeat of Napoleon, the production of lunatic and other unlikely Dauphins was really in King Louis XVIII's interest, discrediting any lingering belief that the real Dauphin might have survived.

The first such Dauphin to surface seems to have been in 1796 when the claim of Jean Marie Hervgault, the son of a Saint Lô tailor, was swiftly dismissed. Then in 1810 a drummer in the garrison at Tortona in Piedmont was sentenced to run the gauntlet three times for some minor infringement. As he was about to be flogged he said he had something important to communicate to the commandant – that he was none other than the Dauphin. He had intended to tell no one except his sister but he could not allow the royal body to be subjected to such a punishment. He was sent by the commandant to Turin where he was, apparently, recognised by an old Swiss retainer at the Palace of Versailles. For some time he was held in awe by what passed for Court circles in Turin, but, later, an inquiry was ordered and he was again sentenced to run the gauntlet three times. The ladies of the Court interceded and the punishment was reduced to one run. As he stripped off his shirt he is said to have exclaimed, 'What an indignity for a Bourbon!' After the whipping he disappeared.

In fact there have been over 100 false claimants to be the Dauphin, including the naturalist John James Audubon, whose writings were claimed by his supporters to have contained clues to his royal status, and a missionary from Wisconsin, Eleazar Williams, who was part

Mohawk Indian. The claimant who went furthest was Karl Wilhelm Naundorff, probably born in 1785 and in 1810 was in Spandau where his parents received Prussian citizenship. In 1824 he was sentenced to three years for counterfeiting. On his release he began to call himself the Duke of Normandy and claimed he had been kidnapped, taken to the US and brought back to Europe. In 1834 he was in Paris to give evidence at the trial of another false Dauphin, the Duke of Richmond. Whilst there he managed to convince a number of members of the court that he was in fact the genuine article. He knew a great deal about the life of the Court, and Louis's childhood nurse, Madame de Rambaud, accepted him as the Dauphin. There were, naturally, some resemblances; he had a large mole on his thigh, a scar on his upper lip, a similar and unusual vaccination mark and protruding teeth. He had also acquired some private knowledge of the Bourbons and knew the structural layout of the Temple. The Dauphin's old governess was also convinced, as was the wife of the shoemaker who had guarded him.

However, Princess Marie Thérèse, his 'sister', refused to acknowledge him and in 1836 he sued her for the return of property he claimed belonged to him. He was promptly deported to England. His support faded away and he died in 1845 in Delft, possibly after being poisoned. His grave has the inscription, 'Here lies Louis XVII, King of France and of Navarre' – in French of course. His heirs struggled on for over a century until the claim was finally dismissed in 1954.

In April 2000 scientists from the University of Münster announced that, after examining samples from a lock of Marie Antoinette's hair and other samples from the real Dauphin's dried heart, the DNA closely matched those of other members of the French royal family.

On 3 April 1817 a very attractive, small woman apparently swam ashore from the Bristol Channel and appeared in Almondsbury in Gloucestershire. She spoke no English but pointed excitedly when she saw a picture of a pineapple. She was taken into care and lodged at Knole Park, the home of magistrate Samuel Worrall. In a matter of weeks she became the protégé of his wife.

The girl certainly behaved strangely. She bathed naked in the lake, refused to drink from a glass until she had washed it herself, spoke a language unlike anything Mrs Worrall or her neighbours had heard and prayed to her God, Alla Tallah.

Eventually all was revealed. Fortunately, a Portuguese seaman, Manuel Enes, who claimed to understand her language, appeared and translated the girl's story. Her name was Caraboo and she was the Princess of the island of Javasu from where she had been abducted by sailors. She had eventually escaped by jumping overboard from the ship she was travelling on.

Mrs Worrall was ecstatic, and visitors flocked to see the Princess use a bow and arrow, fence and, particularly, bathe naked. But unfortunately so did a journalist who wrote her story in the *Bath Chronicle*. Now, a Mrs Neale recognised the Princess as a girl who had been employed by her as a servant and had entertained her children by speaking in a made-up language. Her name was Mary Baker and she came from Devon.

According to various versions of her story she had married a man, Bakerstehndt, and had a child, which died. She had also been the associate of highwaymen before escaping from them. Her parents claimed that she had had rheumatic fever and, from that time on, was not quite right in the head.

The Princess admitted nearly all; Mrs Worrall swallowed her pride and paid her passage to the US from where she returned seven years later. Occasionally she would agree to give performances as the Princess, often in New Bond Street, Bath; but, by now, the novelty of her story had faded. Later in her life she sold leeches to the Bristol Infirmary Hospital. She remarried and in 1829 gave birth to a daughter. She died on 4 January 1865.

OVER THE YEARS there have been many claimants to being the Grand Duchess Anastasia, alleged to have survived the massacre of the Russian royal family in 1917. The story of her survival gathered pace from the fact that the bodies of Anastasia and her brother Alexei were missing when the mass grave was dug up in 1991. But the claims had begun long before that. In 1930 five leaders of a religious sect were sentenced to death at Vovrnech and five others received eight years to be followed by exile for involvement in the impersonation of Anastasia and the general fomentation of disorder. The latter included Anna Sazonova, a former nun, who claimed to be the Grand Duchess.

There have also been a number who have claimed they are Alexei, the son of the Tsar, or at least his son or now his grandson. The more recent have included the Canadian Ernest Veerman who first changed his name to Heino Tammet and then to Alexei Tammet-Romanov. Haemophilia, from which Alexei suffered, is passed through the male line but Tammet-Romanov was not a sufferer. His supporters explained this by saying that Alexei's condition had been misdiagnosed. Tammet-Romanov claimed that both he and Alexei had an undescended testicle, but there the resemblance seems to have ended. He died in June 1977.

In 1998 the newspaper *Pravda* said it knew of at least 80 false Alexeis. That was the year when Oleg Filatov, a Customs inspector from St Petersburg, put forward his claim as heir to the Romanov dynasty. Apparently, according to Oleg, having survived the shooting, Alexei was cured of haemophilia by being fed raw reindeer meat, seal blubber and bear flesh. He then went on to produce a family of which Oleg was a descendant and the rightful claimant.

There are only two women who have made any real success of their claims to be Anastasia. One was Eugenia Smith, or Eugenia Drabek Smetisko, the author of the *Autobiography of HIH Anastasia Nicholaevna of Russia*. Originally she claimed to have been given the manuscript by the Grand Duchess but, after failing a lie-detector test required by the publisher, she decided to become the Grand Duchess herself. Her handwriting did not resemble that of Anastasia nor did her features when compared with photographs, but she put together a good life on the New York cocktail circuit as Anastasia. In 1995 she refused DNA testing which would have substantiated or disproved her claim and died two years later.

The second and the one over whom opinion was more divided was Anna Anderson. In 1920 she was in a psychiatric hospital in Dalldorf, Germany, after being rescued from a canal in Berlin a few weeks earlier. It was here that another patient, reading about the massacre of the Tsar's family, thought there was a strong resemblance between Anastasia and Anna. It was at this point that Anna Tschaikowski, as she then called herself, began a lifetime's work to establish herself as the Grand Duchess Anastasia.

Her story, as Anastasia, was both harrowing and romantic. Left for dead in the cellar at Yekaterinburg she had been smuggled out by two Bolshevik guards named Tschaikowski, one of whom, Alexander, she married in Bucharest and had a baby by him. Other versions have it that Alexander raped her.

The trio survived on the money made from selling uncut emeralds that had been sewn in her dress. Her husband was recognised and assassinated in Bucharest, after which she had a breakdown and the child was taken away. Her brother-in-law, Sergei, then took her to Berlin but soon disappeared; she decided to end it all by jumping into the canal. In fact, there was never a trace of either of the brothers.

In order to establish her claim, there were certain problems to be overcome. First and, in the eyes of many, fatal was the fact that she spoke no Russian. However, she claimed the atrocities made the language offensive to her. There was also a Berlin landlady who knew her as Franziska Schankowska at the time she jumped into the canal, and one of the Schankowskas claimed her as a sister.

On her side, however, were ranged one of the late Tsarina's ladies-in-waiting along with up to a dozen Romanov relatives and Anastasia's French tutor, Pierre Gaillard. Also, she had bunions in the same place as the Grand Duchess, there was skull damage which could have been caused by a rifle butt and a scar on her shoulder in the same place that Anastasia had a mole. There was another scar on her left hand similar to one on the Grand Duchess, which had been caused when a coach door was slammed on it. It was at this time that Anna now took the surname Anderson.

At stake were the Tsar's millions, and in 1933 a German court declared that Anastasia was dead and made over the Tsar's property in Germany to six surviving relatives. In 1938 Anna Anderson brought an action to reverse the court's decision but it was not heard until May 1968 when the judgment went against her. She then went to the US and married a Dr John Manahan.

Anna died in 1984 and in 1995 DNA tests, the bane of an impostor's life, proved conclusively she was not the Grand Duchess. Earlier, there had been a number of books and two films about her, and The HIH Grand Duchess Anastasia Historical Society still exists to advance the theory that Anna Anderson Manahan was indeed the youngest daughter of Tsar Nicholas II.

In 2002 Natalya Bilikhodze, whose exact whereabouts were a secret, was probably the last of the claimants who has surfaced. She was then 101 and was apparently living in Georgia.

THE HUMBERT family, led by the redoubtable Thérèse, flourished in Paris for over three decades at the end of the nineteenth century. During this period she created a whole family of litigants laying claim and counterclaim to the fortune of the non-existent American multi-millionaire Robert Henry Crawford, whom she maintained she had nursed back to health and who had, in gratitude, given her a legacy of $20 million.

She created two nephews, Robert and Henry – in reality her brothers Emile and Romaine – who obtained a court order sealing a safe in which the Crawford money was supposedly being held. The safe was placed in the middle of the Humbert salon during which time Mme Humbert borrowed against its contents. The completely bogus court action she had created spun out Jarndyce-like into an impenetrable web of litigation over the years while Mme Humbert and her family gave the most lavish of parties and balls to le tout Paris who were, apparently, quite under the spell.

Finally, on 9 May 1902, their creditors obtained an order to open the safe while the Humberts were in Madrid. Sadly, but not surprisingly, there was no $20 million, merely around $1,000 along with an empty jewel case, an Italian coin and some brass buttons. The Humberts were arrested in Spain and returned in something approaching triumph from Madrid, being given a sleeping compartment on an express train. Once in prison in the Conciergerie Mme Humbert complained about the cold and a Turkestan carpet was provided for her. As the months went by opinion in France grew in her favour. No one who deceived banks and moneylenders could be really bad. Sentenced to five years' imprisonment and her brothers to three and two years, they did not fare too well. She sorted feathers and the men addressed envelopes. A hoped-for early release did not materialise, possibly because they had no funds to pay lawyers to petition for them. When she was finally released she emigrated to the US, where she died in Chicago in 1918.

What is perhaps the most curious aspect is that the French aristocracy was quite prepared to bow its knee to a woman described as 'short, stout, yellowed skinned, she looked like a typical French cook'. She was almost completely uneducated and spoke with both a lisp and a thick Provençal accent.

SHORTLY AFTER the Humberts, three aristocrats came to grief in Paris after sparkling, if relatively brief, careers. The Marquis de Massa Malaspina, the Baron de Ruelle and the Comtesse de Chatillon had earlier worked the South of France. There the Marquis had a yacht, the *Sibille*, on which his friends could be found regularly. Thinking it would be a lovely idea to host a party for the local gentry where they could listen to music as they cruised in the Mediterranean – as paying guests of course – he borrowed some money to defray the advance expenses. Sadly, on the day of the cruise when the invitees arrived at the harbour they found the Marquis, the Baron and the Comtesse had already weighed anchor. The Comtesse, a handsome woman on the right side of 50 with two eligible daughters, now moved into an apartment in the Avenue de la Grand Armée, Paris, and began entertaining wealthy nobility. One Spaniard was so entranced that he sent home for his sons to come to Paris. He only took fright when the Comtesse began speaking of a safe in the Credit Lyonnais. It was the same trick used by Mme Humbert and the Spaniard beat a hasty retreat.

After that she took up with a German manufacturer to keep the tradespeople at bay. The house of cards toppled when she was traced, along with the false Marquis and Baron, to rooms near the Arc de Triomphe. The Comtesse was in fact Anne Simonet, the daughter of a grocer.

In December 1902 a Countess married the Austrian Prince, Arthurpold Stuart de Modena, in Portsmouth of all unlikely places. There were reasons for a quiet wedding. The Countess was the former wife of the Earl of Russell who had been locked with her in a decade of litigation over conjugal rights, allegations and counter-allegations of cruelty. It had ended badly for the Earl who served a three-month sentence for bigamy, one of the last occasions when a peer was tried by his fellow peers in the House of Lords.

Now the Countess sought happiness with her Austrian Prince. It should have been a simple question of checking references and the Almanac de Gotha existed for just this sort of thing. Unfortunately, while described, when he later appeared in the police court, as being of manly bearing and his occupation noted as that of gentleman, a more accurate description would have been gentleman's valet. William Brown, for that is who he was, had been born the son of a coachman residing in Frimley. He received three months but since he had been in custody awaiting his trial he was released after less than a week. Curiously, the Countess did not seem to mind the deception – that, or it spoke volumes for the charm of the groom – because there was a reconciliation. This did not last long. He beat her and was eventually found in Piccadilly with another lady, although now he was a cavalry officer, Captain Stuart. This time the Countess thought enough was enough.

Even in these more sophisticated times royal conmen still exist. In 2003 Prince Satohito Arisugawa, apparently related to the Emperor of Japan, but really Yasuyuki Kitano the son of a greengrocer, married Harumi Sakamoto, a 47-year-old divorcee, in a lavish ceremony in an exclusive Tokyo club. Present were some 350 guests – businessmen, politicians and actors – who brought with them the traditional wedding gifts of cash in envelopes totalling around £60,000. In fact the Arisugawa family had died out in 1913, and the so-called prince, who had been passing himself off as royalty since 1980, had among other scams sold mineral water bottles emblazoned with the Imperial crest to Shinto shrines. In September 2006 both bride and groom were sent to prison for 26 months for deception. One guest did not bear any resentment, telling reporters, 'I try to remember he gave a country bumpkin like me the fleeting dream of attending a royal wedding.'

Carl von Veltheim

THE GERMAN-BORN Carl Ludwig Kurtze, better known as von Veltheim, plagued South Africa and England, as well as his home country. He was born in Brunswick on 4 December 1857 where his father was a forester's clerk, and by the age of 12 he was on his way, stealing his father's watch and some silver spoons. This was forgiven, but when his father died, he was sent to the Gymnasium (German grammar school) at Blakenburg. At the age of 13 he stole a master's pistol and contrived to shoot himself in the face, which marked him for life. From there he went to an orphanage and then to sea as a cabin boy. In 1872 he deserted and, now as Louis Weder, came to London. In 1880 he was in the German Navy but he stole Freiherr von Veltheim's gold chain, diamond ring and a seal engraved with the von Veltheim arms. This was to be his future identity.

Many women were attracted to him, very often to their cost. In Australia on 19 November 1886 he married Mary Laura Yearsley from Perth. He lived with her until early the next year when he left for South Africa before departing once more to England. It does seem that Mary Laura was his equal when it came to a con. Now she sailed for England, meeting a man on the way. After somehow meeting up again with von Veltheim, together they worked the Badger Game on the poor man. He managed to negotiate a payment of £2,000 to the deceived husband – von Veltheim – down to £750. Then von Veltheim went to Belgium and on to Germany where he relieved a woman of a considerable sum, met up yet again with Mary, and it was off to New York for a spell of high living.

In 1894 he was back again in Europe, leaving Mary in the US. He managed to obtain a temporary appointment as the US Consular Agent for Santa Marta, from where he advertised for a wife in the German newspapers and was contacted by a Paula Schiffer. Meanwhile Mary had turned up in London, where she met up with him again.

He told her he was penniless and had to go back to Germany. There he collected Paula Schiffer, as well as £500 from her, and then they returned to London where he 'married' her at St Giles Registry Office. He collected another £1,000 from her to start a business in the US, but she went home to Germany. He stayed in London spending much of his time involved in schemes against the South African millionaires, Barney Barnato and his nephews, Solly and Woolf, the Joel brothers.

By now von Veltheim had 'married' again. This time the lucky woman was Marie Mavrigordato and he was now Franz Ludwig Platen. He obtained £300 in cash but he was refused more by her trustees. It was then he let slip that the marriage was bigamous and he went into hiding. In April that year he sailed for South Africa and enlisted in the Cape Mounted Police.

In 1900 he was deported from South Africa back to England. From there it was to Trieste for a splendid fraud. In an outrageous version of the Spanish Prisoner Swindle he represented himself as the last survivor of men who had been entrusted with the burial of £1 million belonging to ex-President Kruger. He only needed funds and the opportunity to return to the Transvaal to retrieve it. To this end he raised a considerable amount, giving Bills of Exchange as security. Acclaimed a public benefactor, a bust was cast in his honour.

When he had thoroughly milked the good burghers of Trieste it was off to Nervi where he seduced Henrietta Crodel who was away from her husband, and then it was back to Capri. She did not last long. At the Hotel Pagano he met Maria Carrie Hulse and they began living together in Naples and Sorrento before he persuaded her to go to New York with him where he 'married' her. June 1905 saw a 'marriage' to Ernestine Gauthier on board a transatlantic liner with a friend posing as the priest. In August that year he could be found in Neustadt in the Black Forest, under the alias of Captain Oliver Jackson, taking up with an old flame, Clara Ketterer, whom he promised to marry and from whom he obtained a substantial sum. Two years later she committed suicide. By then he had at least 20 identifiable aliases.

His downfall resulted from a long and complicated vendetta with the Joel family whom he tried to dupe out of £30,000. When he failed, in 1896 he shot and killed Woolf Joel in his office in South Africa. Von Veltheim appeared on 20 July before a Dutch jury when, to the fury of the trial judge, he was acquitted but was immediately rearrested and charged with blackmailing Solly Joel. A month later, on 28 August, the charge was adjourned *sine die* – with no appointed date for resumption – and von Veltheim was deported across the Portuguese border (into present-day Mozambique) as a danger.

He was not done for yet, however. From Delagoa Bay he wrote demanding more money from Solly Joel who sought police protection in London in case von Veltheim should turn up there. Turn up he eventually did via the Transvaal, where he had served four months for breach of the expulsion order, and Natal to which he was then deported. He was thrown out of Natal and sent to Lorenzo Marques.

Arrested there as a vagabond and sent to the Cape, in September 1899 his wanderings temporarily ended with the outbreak of the Boer War. He offered his services as a secret agent to the Boer Government which promptly had him arrested and jailed in Pretoria where he remained for a year until the British released him. After that he returned to England, via Cape Town, when he began to blackmail Solly Joel again.

Von Veltheim was arrested while visiting Paris and extradited to London where he stood trial on 8 February 1908 charged with demanding money with menaces. His defence was that 'the letters were only to frighten Solly Joel and the scare came off. Indeed it did.' He received 20 years' penal servitude but was released on licence after serving 11 and was deported on 11 March 1919.

Imposturing

ONE OF THE GREAT impostors of the 1920s was Stephane Otto who, at times, claimed to be the King of the Belgians. Born in 1899 he spoke five languages and was reputed to drink only champagne. On the plus side he was awarded a Croix de Guerre during the First World War. On the minus side he appeared in a variety of guises including the son of the French poet Maurice Maeterlinck.

In 1919 posing as a member of the Belgian General Staff, he pinned the Grand Cross of the Order of Leopold on Major General H.T. Allen, Commanding Officer of the American Army of the Occupation of the Rhine. Three months later he was in the dock convicted of wearing a uniform without authority. He then joined the French Foreign Legion from which he deserted to pursue an actress.

In Perpignan, he received 50 days' imprisonment for impersonating Lord Ashton, 'the representative of the Prince of Wales'. He had already been deported from England when, in 1927, he appeared in Crewe magistrates' court charged with a variety of offences including obtaining 12s. 6d. from a clergyman. He was wearing the uniform of a French naval officer and received 9 months' imprisonment. In 1929 he committed suicide at the age of 30, jumping from the third floor of a lodging house in Brussels.

The Great Pretender

In 1802 Mary Robinson, then aged about 15, the so-called 'Maid of Buttermere', in the Lake District, was the last woman to fall into the clutches of the gentleman–swindler John Hatfield.

Hatfield had earlier married the niece of the Marquis of Granby whom he deserted to go and live in London, running up debts and forging drafts. On this occasion the Duke of Rutland, who was a distant relative, was persuaded to pay them off. In 1784 Hatfield re-emerged as a relative of the Viceroy of Dublin, working the same scams. The Duke again settled his debts, but he did not do so a third time when Hatfield was arrested in Scarborough and received eight years.

It is amazing how many confidence men in prison attract otherwise sensible women. Representing himself as a wronged aristocrat, he next conned a Mrs Nation into paying his debts and marrying him when he was released in 1800. Almost immediately he began another swindle and went on the run. He arrived in Buttermere where Mary, daughter of the owner of the Fish Hotel, had already been admired for her beauty by the Lakeland poets, and in particular by Wordsworth in *The Prelude*.

There was no way Hatfield could press his suit until he had transformed himself into the Hon. Alexander Augustus Hope, MP for Linlithgow and brother of the Earl of Hopetoun. Now the pair were married on 2 October 1802 and Samuel Taylor Coleridge reported the event for the London papers. Almost immediately the game was up. On 6 November, the *Sun* reported that the real Augustus Hope was abroad and that Hatfield was already married.

He went on the run to Swansea where he was arrested and tried for the crime of personation – what would today be identity fraud – at Carlisle Assizes. He was hanged on 3 September 1803. One account of the execution has him explaining to the hangman how the rope should be placed. Mary later married a Richard Harrison and ran the Fish Inn before moving to Caldbeck where she died on 7 February 1837.

ONE OF THE current crop of impostors is Frederic Bourdin who has had up to 40 false identities. He was born in 1974 but has the ability to look years younger than his true age. He has been a tiger hunter, a rich British tourist, a college lecturer and a businessman, but his main speciality over the years has been the impersonation of orphans and long-lost sons. In 1977 he was Nicholas Barclay, the lost son of a San Antonio, Texas family, claiming he had escaped from a child prostitution ring. When the boy's parents went to Spain to identify their son in the US embassy, so keen were they to believe in him that it did not matter that Bourdin spoke with a French accent and that their son's eyes had changed colour. He lived with them for three months before a DNA test proved him an impostor. Released from a six-year sentence, he moved to Grenoble where he was another lost son, Leo Balley, who had been missing since 1996. Again a DNA test proved otherwise.

In Spain in 2004 he was Ruben Sanchez Espinoza whose mother had been killed in the Madrid bombing. When he was exposed he was deported to France. However, the following year, he became 15-year-old Francisco Hernandes-Fernandez whose parents had been killed in a car accident. By now he was becoming bald, a problem he solved by wearing a woollen cap day and night. He had enrolled at a college in Pau, France, telling the head teacher that he had bad scars which he wished to hide. Instead of shaving he was using depilatory creams. He spent a month there before another teacher recognised him from a television programme and in September 2006 he received four months' imprisonment.

ONE OF THE more harmless impostors was the Latvian-born Harry Domela. His father and brothers were killed in the First World War and Domela moved to Germany where he reinvented himself as Baron Korff. After a few short prison sentences he went to

Heidelberg where he became Prince Lieven of Latvia. He closely re-sembled Prince Wilhelm of Hohenzollern, grandson of the deposed Kaiser, and he certainly was not going to correct this impression when he was mistaken for him. Although he was royally entertained by local businessmen and dignitaries, he never seems to have asked for money, or been given any for that matter. However, his presence began to attract press attention and he decided to join the French Foreign Legion. He was arrested boarding a train to France.

While awaiting trial he wrote his memoirs *The Sham Prince*, and, on his acquittal, when the court ruled in his favour, they sold well, as did the film rights. There were two plays written about him, in one of which he played himself. With some of the proceeds he bought a small cinema in Berlin which showed him starring in the film version of his memoirs. In 1933 he went to live as Victor Zsajka in the Nether-lands and there met the literati. He fought in the Republican army during the Spanish Civil War. He was later interned in Vichy France, and when the Second World War ended he went to Mexico with the help of the writer André Gide, before going on to Venezuela where he became a teacher. He disappeared from view in 1978.

In 2005 a man claiming he was the Earl of Buckingham was stopped over a passport irregularity when he tried to board a cross-Channel ferry in Calais. It took many months to unravel his story. Certainly the identity was false. In 1982 he had obtained the birth certificate of a baby, Charles Edward Buckingham, who had died in a road accident.

On 8 November 2005 he received 21 months, reduced on appeal to nine. Meanwhile efforts continued to discover his true identity. There were suggestions he might be an East German spy or an American naval intelligence officer who disappeared in the 1980s, but in fact he turned out to be Charles Albert Stopford III, a US Navy sailor from Florida, the son of a Methodist minister. He had carried out the deception for over 20 years, and his wife and children, who had believed his story that he was educated at Harrow and Cambridge, were said to be hurt but intrigued to discover his real identity.

FOR SHEER variety, the fraudulent exploits of Horatio Buckland take some beating. The son of a respected clerk of works in south London, Buckland joined the Grenadier Guards in 1884, but army life did not suit him. He was a repeated deserter, serving short sentences and then being compulsorily re-enlisted. He finally deserted in 1888, after which he promoted the Klondyke Prospecting Company. The next year he had a mechanical engineering company giving lessons to students; then it was camping on the Welsh hills for 30 shillings a week, after which he was Lord Armstrong's land agent. Then he organised trips to Spithead to see the Naval Review for which he wanted a steward and stewardess who had to pay £50 as a deposit for their honesty. There was of course nothing to prospect, no lessons were given, no tents in Wales, he was nobody's land agent, and while there was certainly a Naval Review, he was nowhere near it. Having convinced people to part with their money, he would move on to the next scam. There were more charges of fraud and one of bigamy for which he received 18 months; after that he became a bogus coal merchant and received five years in 1904. Two years earlier he was assisting the Russians and being paid £200 for every collier captured during their war with Japan. In 1909 he persuaded a firm that he could erect portable ice rinks and in January the next year he received three years. He wrote to the authorities from prison saying he had information about a gang of blackmailing pederasts and although he did not fancy the role of sodomite he was willing to infiltrate them if he was released. The authorities were not deceived. From then he faded from view.

ONE OF THE most engaging conwomen of the nineteenth century was the Irish-born Eliza Gilbert. At 15, apparently about to be married off by her mother to an elderly judge, she promptly eloped with Thomas James, an officer in the East India Company who, within weeks, she cordially loathed. Sent back to England from India she began a shipboard romance with another officer, Thomas Lennox. Now an outcast from polite society, she created a new image for herself as Doña Maria Dolores Porris y Montez, Lola Montez, a Spanish aristocrat, sometimes the daughter of a General, sometimes his widow. Despite the fact she spoke only rudimentary Spanish, she carried on the deception for the rest of her life, during which she married bigamously at least twice, became the mistress of Franz Liszt and the nemesis of King Ludwig I of Bavaria who was infatuated with her. That is when she was not, for one reason or another, living under the names of Betty or Eva James, Rosanna Gilbert, Betty or Betsy Watson, Mlle Marie Marie, Mrs Burton or Fanny Gibbons.

BORN IN 1964 David Hampton, the son of a Buffalo lawyer, trained as a dancer. He began his career as a conman in 1983 when he and a friend were refused entry to New York's fashionable Studio 54. They returned to their hotel, hired a limousine and reappeared at the nightclub pretending Hampton was the son of Sidney Poitier and his friend the son of Gregory Peck. They were invited in as celebrities. From then on he became David Poitier and, using a purloined address book, he talked his way into the homes of the great and the good, including Melanie Griffith and Calvin Klein, often claiming he had been mugged and repaying them with tales of his famous 'actor–father'. After his seventh arrest in October 1983 he was imprisoned for 21 months, and his story became the basis of the play *Six Degrees of Separation*. He heard of the play's first night, gate-crashed the party and promptly claimed $100 million compensation. He failed in his suit and then, issuing death threats, hounded the playwright John Guare. He was later acquitted on a charge of harassment. For the remainder of his life he continued to play the part of David Poitier, sometimes wriggling out of arrests by suggesting that someone was impersonating him. He died in July 2003 of an AIDS-related illness.

SIR ROGER CHARLES Doughty Tichbourne apparently died when the sailing ship *Bella* sank between Rio de Janeiro and Jamaica in 1854. Tichbourne was the heir to a baronetcy, and although he was officially declared dead in 1855 his mother could not accept this. When the then baronet died in 1862 she began a campaign to find her long-lost son, placing advertisements worldwide in newspapers.

Her efforts were rewarded when Arthur Orton, then calling himself Castro and working as a butcher in Wagga Wagga, Australia, came forward to claim the title. Tichbourne, a cultured man, had weighed some 125 pounds at his death and Orton was a massive 300 pounds, but, after all, Tichbourne had not been seen for 14 years and could have changed. Letters were exchanged, and an elderly black servant, Bogle, who had known Roger well was gulled into believing Orton was indeed the long-lost heir. Money was sent to Orton to come to England with his family where Lady Tichbourne welcomed him. Others were not convinced; he spoke no French, tattoos that Tichbourne had were no longer visible and he knew nothing about his old school. Nevertheless, in 1871, 100 people at the trial over the inheritance claimed that he was indeed Tichbourne. In the witness box he made a poor showing, maintaining that he had suffered memory loss whenever a difficult question arose. Although there is no doubt he had a good knowledge of some of the Tichbourne affairs – learned, it was alleged, from letters Lady Tichbourne had written to him – the case went against him.

After another trial in 1873 lasting some six months, it was found he was wanted under the name Orton for horse stealing in Australia, and he received 14 years for perjury. On his release, after 11 years, he toured the music halls with decreasing success and he finally opened a tobacconist's shop in Kilburn. In 1895 he published his 'confessions' in the People. He died destitute in Shouldham Street, Marylebone, on 1 April 1898 at the age of 64. His coffin was inscribed 'Sir Roger Charles Doughty Tichbourne'. Curiously, two days before his death a collection of papers relating to the case, including posters advertising his lecture tours, had been sold at auction by Knight, Frank & Rutley for a total sum of £7 17s. 6d. His wife died in 1925 in a workhouse in Southampton where she was known as Lady Tichbourne.

Ellen Peck

U NTIL SHE WAS 51, Ellen Peck seems to have led a blameless life. Then, tiring of domesticity in Sparkville, New York, she moved to Gotham itself. By all accounts she was physically well preserved, and in 1878 had little difficulty in ensnaring the elderly and lustful B.T. Babbitt who had made his fortune from soap. Invited to his mansion she stole $10,000 in negotiable bonds. She then volunteered to act as his personal detective in his hunt for the thief, when in fact, she had already sold the bonds. In normal circumstances she would not expect any recompense but, 'as she had only her widow's pension', the old fool gave her $5,000 to begin the search and later wrote her another cheque for a similar amount. By the time he hired proper detectives she was back in Sparkville where she was arrested. Sentenced to four years she was paroled in a year, and now Dr Jason Marks was persuaded to part with $20,000 in cash and jewellery. In 1887 it was the turn of Jay Gould who, as a friend of Inspector Thomas Byrnes, certainly should have known better.

It was Marks who had her arrested and charged but she was released in 1892. Two more years in Sparkville and she was bored again. So, from a Brooklyn Hotel she became Mary Hansen, the wife of an Admiral in the Danish Navy, and was able to persuade banks to advance her up to $50,000. Then it was into a house where the 80-year-old Dr Christopher Lott was taken to her bed, for which privilege he was taken for $10,000. Lott clearly thought his money had been reasonably well spent because he said of her, 'She was the last craving of my life.' The roll call was endless: she took $4,000 from Nellie Shea, a nurse she had installed to look after the exhausted Lott and there were allegations of 'an unnatural and unwholesome liaison'. Her former lawyer was another of her victims.

She was not averse to helping the police if it suited her, and her collaboration in 1887 with Inspector Byrnes led to the arrest of Julius Columbani, a friend of the forger Louis Siscovitch and Louis's brother, the notorious and lethal Carlos.

In 1897 it was five years in Auburn jail again for fraud, and, after a short period of recuperation up country, it was back to New York where John Grady was persuaded that Ms Peck's kitchen cupboard was a better place than his safe to keep diamonds worth some $21,000. Facing an indictment of 25 counts this remarkable woman was acquitted.

Swindles on other men followed until in 1907 she was sent away again. An appeal was rejected in 1909 but she was pardoned the following year. She was then 82 years of age. Retirement was never a consideration. In 1913, the year she died, she seduced a Latin American businessman bound for Vera Cruz. So enamoured was he that he signed over at least one plantation to her.

Military manoeuvres

IN 1916 A DESERTER from the Black Watch regiment, Thomas Henry Henshall, awarded himself the Victoria Cross along with the Distinguished Conduct Medal, the Military Medal and the Russian Order of St George. He toured towns in the Midlands, his 'empty' sleeve showing four gold stripes. He had obtained the ribbons from a pawnbroker in Liverpool. In Barnsley he sold a German helmet at a charity bazaar to a Colonel Hewitt for £3 who promptly gave it back to him. In Chester, he addressed an audience at the Royalty Theatre on recruiting, and fooled a chaplain at New Brighton into announcing him as holding the Victoria Cross. In Leeds he was on crutches; at Birkenhead he gave parties to tradesmen and left without paying. Eventually, a police officer, visiting him in a temperance hotel in Barnsley, put his hand inside Henshall's shirt and found the missing arm. Twelve months' hard labour.

WEARING unearned medals is not enough for some conmen. Their actions have to be more meritorious than the last person. One whose claims reached the highest level was Australian Danny Robert Shakespeare, also known as Michael Paggett, who claimed that during his time as an SAS officer he had shot Osama bin Laden in the foot. More prosaically, in March 2005 he was arrested at a Coorparoo club, Queensland, for swindling business women.

TEN YEARS before Henshall, in October 1906, William Voigt, a 57-year-old shoemaker, petty criminal and swindler, bought a second-hand uniform of a Captain in the Prussian Guards six months after his last release from prison. Now, suitably dressed, he strolled around Berlin acknowledging the salutes he received from regular soldiers.

On 16 October he marched into an army barracks and ordered ten soldiers to follow him on an important mission: a trip on the railway to Köpenick. On their arrival he ordered them to arrest mayor Langerhans on suspicion of fraud. When the man dared to ask why, Voigt told him he was acting under orders. He had the town's treasurer, Rosenkranz, bring him the town's books for him to examine; he confiscated them and 4,000 marks for which he signed a receipt. He then ordered two carriages and sent the mayor and treasurer under military guard to Berlin where, since no one expected them, they were quickly released. He returned to the city by train, discarding his uniform in a carriage.

He was caught ten days later when he tried to obtain a passport to allow him to leave Germany. He was sentenced to four years' imprisonment for forgery and impersonating an officer but was pardoned after two, possibly to save the Prussian army from further ridicule. From then on the 'Captain of Köpenick' toured Europe and the US as a highly successful cabaret-cum-lecture act before he retired to Luxembourg on a pension given to him by a Berlin widow. He died, ruined by post-First World War inflation, on 3 January 1922.

On the strength of his personality, American Joseph A. Cafasso, seemingly a gruff barrel-chested military man who claimed he had won the Silver Star for bravery and served in Vietnam as well as being part of the failed mission to rescue hostages in Iran in 1980, was hired by the Fox News Channel for whom he worked as a military pundit for four months. In fact his total military experience was 44 days of basic camp training at Fort Dix in May and June 1976. Before he conned Fox he sold spurious stories to the *New York Times* of a former Russian officer who had fled to avoid killing Chechnyan civilians.

Born in 1956 in New Jersey, Cafasso graduated from Carteret High School and over the years became an associate of Rear Admiral Clarence A. Hill Jnr, once a colleague of Rear Admiral John M. Poindexter, the former National Security Advisor. Cafasso had persuaded Hill that he had information on flight TWA 800, allegedly shot down by a missile when it crashed off Long Island in July 1996. Through Hill he was introduced to a number of retired generals as well as American and Serbian activists. He also worked with the failed Presidential campaign of Patrick J. Buchanan, and later he worked for a number of radio stations including WABC in New York.

In 2003, under a different name, he was still carrying off the deception that he was a senior figure in US military intelligence. Over a period of some four months he deceived a New York lawyer – whom he had met over the Internet – with his tales of derring-do, explaining his frequent disappearances and absences as being due to national security. Fortunately, on this occasion her only losses were her pride and a telephone bill for some $300.

The New York lawyer was fortunate to escape so lightly. Mary Smith* fared terribly at the hands of William Jordan whom she also met on an Internet dating site in November 2000. Almost immediately the deception started with Jordan disappearing for weeks at a time. She checked him out and found he was a director of Endeavour Marketing in East Lothian. Listed as a co-director was a Julie Jones*.

Ms Smith* drove to East Lothian and found Jordan at a house with children's toys in the garden. Jordan then, apparently, made several telephone calls and received permission to tell her all. He explained that he was a US intelligence agent and this was a safe house where Julie, also an agent, lived. The toys belonged to Julie's children from a former relationship. This explained his secrecy and absences.

In June 2001 he and Mary planned to get married but it was postponed when Jordan told her he was being sent to Israel for five months. He returned for 24 hours and then again went to Israel sending her emails, apparently through the official department of the CIA. He had, he said, been trapped in Jenin, a Palestinian refugee camp, during a massacre there. But now he had decided to leave the CIA, warning her it might be a long and involved process.

It was also an expensive process for her. She obtained credit cards, remortgaged her flat and, finally sold it for a profit of £65,000, which she gave to Jordan. In 2004 she became pregnant by him but he was, he said, now in grave danger and disappeared. When he returned it was with Denise Brown*, another CIA agent. In December 2005 the wheels began to come off when he was interviewed by the police over the misuse of a credit card. Then in January 2006 he warned Mary that he was likely to be arrested on a false charge of bigamy and failing to register as a sex offender. He explained that he had been infiltrated into the offenders' wing of a prison on a bogus charge to get high-level information from a sex offender. Then he had been

* These names have been changed.

told the 'charge' had been dropped but his masters were irritated that he had tried to leave the CIA.

Eventually Mary spoke with Julie, to whom Jordan had actually been married for 16 years, and found each of them had been told the other was a CIA agent. He had also been having a relationship with Denise whom he had again met on the Internet. Quite apart from her self-esteem Mary Smith also lost £188,000.

In December 2006 Jordan pleaded guilty to bigamy, fraud and failure to register as a sex offender. He was sentenced to five years' imprisonment.

IN 2004 ROBERT Hendy-Freegard was convicted of persuading people that they were on an IRA hit list and, at the same time, relieving them of a total of nearly £700,000. His victims were lured into his non-existent spy network, living in so-called safe houses and going on missions.

It all began in 1992 when he was working in The Swan in Newport, Shropshire, where he became friends with two women and a man, students from the nearby Harper Adams Agricultural College. Hendy-Freegard told the man he was an MI5 agent infiltrating an IRA cell in the college. The unfortunate man allowed himself to be beaten up to prove he was tough enough to work with Hendy-Freegard. Later he was told his cover had been blown and that he must disappear. Hendy-Freegard then told the women that the man had cancer and they should all go on a 'farewell tour' of England. He then told them that they were all in danger and should go into hiding and distance themselves from their friends and family. The two women supported Hendy-Freegard, one becoming his lover and they had two children. He also persuaded the man and his parents to pay him over £300,000 to ensure the man's safety.

Hendy-Freegard also took on a newly married personal assistant, seduced her and, again using the IRA as a pretext, cut her off from friends and family. She was made to undergo tests of loyalty such as pretending to be a Jehovah's Witness, spending nights sleeping at Heathrow Airport and on park benches.

In 2000 he relieved a lawyer of £14,000 from her building society account and, among other things, he told her a car she was leasing had been stolen by the Polish mafia. Two years later he obtained some £80,000 from an American child psychologist, telling her that he had infiltrated a criminal network, killed one of its members and was now in hiding. She too had to undergo loyalty tests, which included hiding in a bathroom for three weeks. A woman from Newcastle gave him £16,000 over a period of years to buy off IRA killers released under the Good Friday agreement.

Eventually he was caught in a joint FBI–Scotland Yard operation, in which the telephone of the American child psychologist's parents was bugged, with their co-operation. During a bugged conversation, her mother told Hendy-Freegard she would hand over a further £10,000, but only in person. She met him at Heathrow where he was arrested.

He denied all charges, maintaining his story was true and the arrest was part of a conspiracy against him. Found guilty, a life sentence for kidnapping was quashed in April 2007. On the fraud charges, he received nine years' imprisonment.

Rather less dangerous, perhaps because he posed as a police rather than an army officer, was Michael Hammond who received four and a half years on 4 February 2005 at Isleworth Crown Court. By then the 36-year-old had racked up over 100 offences, mostly for fraud and deception. On 17 May 2004 he was caught on CCTV in the grounds of Windsor Castle pretending to be a senior police officer, saying he was accompanying friends of the princes who did not wish to use the main gate. After he was arrested, he claimed the royal family would welcome his behaviour as it demonstrated how lax security could be.

Over the years he had made 133 hoax calls to the police claiming he needed assistance or reporting sightings of criminals and murder suspects. Once, when he had called up posing as a surgeon fighting heavy traffic to get to a hospital to save a child's life, he had been given a motorcycle escort. Apart from posing as a detective, his other impersonations included a film producer and a polo player, both of which gave him entry into the world of actors and celebrities.

'Gentleman' George Barton

I N 1908 'GENTLEMAN' George Barton was sentenced to death for the killing of James P. McCann in St Louis, Missouri. Far from being of noble birth, a role he played throughout his life, he was the son of a cab driver, born in Tunbridge Wells. At the age of 10, he was sent to a reformatory for five years.

This did him no good at all. At the age of 16, he cracked a safe and stole £2,000. This time he received ten years but the sentence was reduced by the Home Secretary. In fact he was helped by Austin Bidwell, the American who had attempted to rob the Bank of England and who continued his career as a forger while in prison. Barton's pleas for early release had gone unanswered until Bidwell forged two letters informing him that a rich uncle had died and left him £160,000 in cash and 16,000 acres for growing cotton in India; he was needed at once to look after the estate. The letters were smuggled out and duly posted back to the prison. Barton submitted a new petition and was released. He was not out long before he did another burglary and received another ten years, which was then followed by a further 12 years at Lewes Assizes for receiving.

He went to New York in 1891 as Lord Barrington where he gave fine dinners; his taste in wines was excellent and he had a 'way with the ladies which was irresistible'. He married Celestine Miller, the daughter of a rich widow, robbed her of everything and disappeared.

He was next found back in Brighton where he defrauded everyone in sight and burgled his neighbour's home. He took a great interest in helping the police, providing several useful clues until a Scotland Yard detective recognised him as a ticket-of-leave man [a prisoner who has been given early release with conditions] who had failed to report for several months. When the property from the burglary was found at his home he received another 12 years.

On his release he went back to the US where he married the

daughter of a wealthy coal merchant from Philadelphia, stole $800 and abandoned her in Pittsburgh. He married again, this time as Lt Colonel Frederick Neil Barrington, nephew of the Marquess of Abergavenny. The marriage did not last long because the bride's brother made enquiries about the half-colonel's real status and kicked him down a flight of stairs as a result. He then worked in a bar before being taken up by the horse dealer James McCann who appointed him his betting commissioner. Later Barton lured him to a lonely spot and beat him to death. The motive was money again. He had persuaded McCann that he had money coming to him from Britain and obtained an advance against it. It was easier to kill Mc-Cann than repay the loan. Sentenced to hang, he was reprieved and sent to Missouri State Penitentiary, where he had dozens of women visitors. One of the women he charmed was an Englishwoman, Lilian E. Gates who laboured for many years under the delusion that he was not Barton at all but a man, Seymour, who had been her neighbour in England. In 1913 Barton applied for parole and Mrs Gates wrote to Scotland Yard seeking their help in correcting this great injustice since she knew full well that he had been sent by the British Government to infiltrate one of the Irish societies in St Louis.

Barton had also half convinced the US authorities that there might be some doubt as to his identity. A letter from L.B. Hurgel of the penitentiary to Scotland Yard said that Barton claimed the British Government had paid $2,000 to help clear his name and to try to get parole. At the time of his arrest he had said he was on a secret mission but had refused to say what it was. Would Scotland Yard confirm this to be correct and could they send a copy of Barton's fingerprints and Bertillon measurements (a system of measuring facial features used to identify criminals)? Meanwhile Barton had found a witness, Jack Bennett, to say he had seen McCann alive and well in San Francisco a year after his disappearance.

However, the fingerprints and Bertillon measurements settled things as far as the penitentiary was concerned. Thanking Scotland Yard for the documents, Hurgel wrote that Barton was still denying having been in prison in England but, '... he is the only one that thinks so and I don't think he will ever have a chance to be paroled out of this Institution unless he acknowledges his part'. He appears to have been released in about 1918, after which he returned to England. His was one of the many names put forward – with no evidence to support it – as being Jack the Ripper.

Leap of faith

N 1792 **JOANNA** Southcott, a 42-year-old farmer's daughter, proclaimed that she would be giving birth to the Second Messiah. The gestation, which would take ten years, generated an enormous following with supporters, or Southcottians as they liked to be known, totalling over 100,000. Later, 19 October 1814 was announced as the date when the Messiah would be born and, amazingly, 17 out of 21 doctors who examined this 64-year-old woman announced she was indeed pregnant. On the day of the proposed birth, crowds massed in Manchester Street, London, where she now lived. Three died during the vigil which sadly produced no Saviour, and within ten weeks Joanna herself died of a brain disease. She did, however, leave the legacy of a box to be opened 100 years after her death which, she said, would solve a great human crisis. Despite pleas from the dwindling band of supporters, now known as the Panacea Society, the Archbishop of Canterbury refused to allow it to be opened at the beginning of the First World War. When it was opened in 1927, in the presence of the Bishop of Grantham, it was found to contain a lady's nightcap, a horse-pistol, a 1796 lottery ticket, a 1793 French

calendar and, perhaps the most unusual item, a novel entitled *The Surprises of Love*. Her supporters maintained the wrong box had been opened.

During her lifetime Joanna Southcott had kept a certain seal in her possession which ensured those who believed in her powers would go straight to heaven. Replicas were sold at a guinea each and more than 14,000 were produced.

ONE OF JOANNA Southcott's disciples was the confidence trickster and abortionist Mary Bateman who had been looking for a way of making serious money for some years. For a time she considered the dubious attractions of Richard Brothers who styled himself 'The Nephew of Jesus Christ' but she turned away from his preaching. In January 1806 she produced an egg, on which was inscribed 'Crist is coming', which she said had been laid by her hen that morning. Joanna Southcott, whom Bateman had met in 1803, wrote a poem in tribute and after that the obliging hen laid suitably inscribed eggs to order.

Mary Bateman also ran what was called a Brass Screw Racket. Four brass screws and four golden guineas were required to screw down enemies of her customers – the mark paid the four golden guineas and received the brass screws in return. Quite how she achieved this was never fully revealed but some of her clients must have been satisfied. Rebecca Perigo, seemingly with an endless string of enemies, handed over the guineas no less than 17 times, until her husband finally threatened to go to the police. Mary countered this with a white powder mixed with arsenic to be put in the Perigo Yorkshire pudding, with which she was able to 'guarantee to avert a great calamity'.

Mary Bateman was hanged, in a white dress, for Rebecca Perigo's murder in March 1809, completely unrepentant and steadfast in the knowledge that with one of Southcott's seals in her possession she was going straight to heaven. There was even a rumour in the 20,000 strong crowd that an angel would actually come from heaven and either save her or take her away. No angel appeared and, on a more earthly level, a local undertaker charged threepence to view Mary Bateman in her coffin.

IT IS DIFFICULT to categorise the beautiful Anais Chirch from Menilmontant near Paris. Of minor talent, she nevertheless flourished as something of a professional mourner at the Père Lachaise cemetery where, dressed in black, she attended funerals claiming to know the deceased. In May 1904 she so impressed one widower with her tale of how she knew and treasured his wife that they went off to dinner together. This was such a comfort to him in his bereavement that they went on to the Moulin de la Galette dance hall in Montmartre, shortly after which he discovered the loss of all his money. When the police raided her home it was found to be stuffed with prayer books, crucifixes and other religious paraphernalia.

ONE OF THE oldest religious swindles has been the sale of Bibles 'ordered' by the deceased a few days before their death. Percy Willingdon took the deception one step further. He claimed the deceased, usually a clergyman, had not ordered a Bible for his nearest and dearest but instead had ordered a quantity of pornography. Willingdon and his protégé Frank Ross would write a letter pretending that he did not know of the vicar's death and enclosing a bill for £50 or £100. Willingdon was eventually caught when he claimed a vicar who had been paralysed for some years had ordered the saucy pictures. He jumped his bail and went to South America. For his part Ross claimed that no case 'ever came to court'.

In the last few years the scam has been revived when solicitors acting for executors have received invoices for Bibles priced at just under £25. It costs the estate less to pay out than for correspondence to investigate whether the money is really due.

IN THE DAYS before the Second World War when sex education was negligible, advertisements were placed in popular papers:

> To those young men and women who are about to marry here is a little book that no young man or woman should be without. Send 5 shillings and we will send you in plain cover this world famous book.

For their money applicants were sent a ninepenny Bible.

Wʜᴇɴ ᴛʜᴇ vicar failed to appear for the wedding of Rod Earnshaw and Shirley Watson in Huddersfield in August 1996, a first-year student at Lampeter College, intended to be a server at the marriage, stepped in and officiated. The groom later commented, 'I thought the lad looked a bit young but he was incredibly believable.'

Eᴠᴇʀʏ ᴄᴇɴᴛᴜʀʏ produces at least one 'end of the world' scam. Towards the end of the eighteenth century the Prussian gamekeeper Hans Rosenfeld claimed Christianity was a deception and that he would depose King Frederick the Great, ruling in his place with a Council of Twenty-Four Elders. Seven Messianic Seals would then be opened by seven Angels of the Seals. For the leader, the best part of most of the scams is that followers must be prepared to offer their wives and daughters to the great glory of being the leader's mistresses. One man who provided three of his daughters and then found the end of the world endlessly delayed persuaded the King to take action against Rosenfeld who, far from using his self-proclaimed supernatural powers in retaliation, ended his life in prison.

Oʀɪᴄ Bovᴀʀ was born in 1917 and had been an opera coach, actor and mail-order astrologer. Shortly before his death he changed from being a benevolent guru leading a small but distinguished flock, which at one time included the actress Bernadette Peters, to being a mad Messiah. It was during this period that he arranged marriages on sight, had followers watch him create a star and in the summer of 1976 announced that, since he was Jesus, Christmas Day would in future be celebrated on 29 August. He also took to calling himself, 'My Son, Oric Bovar' and repeatedly watching *The Exorcist*.

That summer he and five disciples, who included a teacher and a speed reader, announced they would bring 29-year-old cancer victim Stephanos Hatzitheodorou back to life. They rented his flat and for the next two months chanted, 'Rise, Stephan, rise, rise, rise' – unsurprisingly, to no great effect.

Eventually someone giving her name as Mary Magdalene called the police. Bovar was due to appear in court charged with offences under the health regulations when, on 14 April 1977, after announcing he would step from a tenth-floor window, flutter and return, instead crashed to the ground.

Ferdinand Waldo Demara

I**T WAS NOT FOR** nothing that the identity thief Ferdinand Waldo Demara was known as 'The Great Impostor'. Born in Lawrence, Massachusetts, in 1921 he joined the army at the age of 20 and lasted barely a year. He took the name of a fellow soldier, faked his death and then, as Robert Linton French, became a psychologist. When caught he served 18 months.

From then on he became, among other professions, a civil engineer, an assistant prison warden, a hospital orderly, a cancer researcher, editor, university lecturer and both a Trappist and Benedictine monk. In all his positions he was well regarded by his fellow workers.

His most celebrated manifestation was in March 1951 when he joined the Canadian Navy as the surgeon Dr Joseph Cyr. A great success, he performed a number of operations at the naval hospital

at HMCS *Stadacona*. In June that year he was sent to Korea where he claimed to have extracted a bullet from the lung of a South Korean guerrilla. It was his undoing. The story was reported in the Canadian press and the real Dr Cyr began making enquiries.

In October 1951 he was sent back to Canada in disgrace but he was not charged and instead was deported to the US. He sold his story to *Life* magazine and, for a time, worked in a series of legitimate jobs. But then, once more faking his credentials, he obtained a position in Huntsville Prison, Texas. In 1956 as Mart D. Godgart he taught English, French and Latin in a school in Maine and as a result served a few months for fraud.

In 1967 he obtained a graduation certificate in Bible studies from Multnomah School of the Bible. He then dropped out of sight and died of heart failure on 8 June 1982. He had been working as a Baptist minister in Orange County, California.

In 1960 he had appeared in a cameo role as a surgeon in *The Great Impostor*, a film of his life in which he was played by Tony Curtis. He also played a doctor in *The Hypnotic Eye*.

Is there a doctor in the house?

I N 1906 WHEN Ernest Miller was sentenced to 18 months with hard labour at London's Clerkenwell Sessions for the theft of a watch and chain, the court was told that he worked in the popular music-hall act of Dr Walford Brodie who pretended to cure the disabled. Miller would be brought on stage each night and hop about after being cured. The next night he would be carried on again. As the week went on he became worse and the doctor's cure the greater.

Born in Aberdeen on 11 June 1869 Samuel Murphy Brodie took his name from his brother-in-law H. Werner Walford who was manager of the Connaught Theatre of Varieties in Norwich. Billed as The Laird of Macduff, and possessing self-awarded medical degrees from a variety of universities including Chicago, Brodie toured the music halls with a huge company claiming to cure the afflicted. He also ran the Brodie Electric Drug Company in Blackfriars Road as well as Electric Life Pills and Electric Liniment.

Brodie, who claimed to be an FRMS (a Fellow of the Royal Meteorological Society) advertised in his show that he would, 'Give advice free to the helpless and paralysed. God Save the King!' As part of his act he offered ten shillings per half-minute to anyone who could sit in an electrically wired chair. This feat was accomplished at the Palace Theatre, Blackburn, in 1906 by a James Wright who with the help of friends had bound himself in copper. He sat in the chair until the irate Brodie had him bundled off stage and taken to the dressing room where he was stripped and searched. He was then brought back on stage and exposed as a trickster. Wright claimed damages for false imprisonment and was awarded £3.

Brodie was in the courts again in 1909, this time when Charles Irving, a former assistant, sued for damages for alleged misrepresentation. He had paid £1,000 to the doctor to learn mesmerism, hypnotism, bloodless surgery and 'medical electricity'. Now he complained

that as part of the act he had been made to dress up as a sailor and had been given the wrong medals to wear. Brodie did not do well in the case:

> COUNSEL (quoting): 'In the US I took my degree of doctor of dental surgery.' Is that a lie?
> BRODIE: Oh, it's a showman's privilege.
> COUNSEL: You have continually represented yourself as an MD have you not?
> BRODIE: No, only on one occasion. It means Merry Devil. Theatrical Managers call me that.

The jury awarded Irving his £1,000.

The claim by Brodie that he was a doctor led to an attack by students on 12 November 1909 at the Coliseum, Glasgow. He and his wife Jeannie – who appeared as Princess Rubie and would seemingly be electrocuted by Brodie and then revived – were pelted with eggs and vegetables.

For a time the case did not really cause Brodie any great professional harm, but as the years went by and people learned more about electricity his popularity waned. His wife, her sister and his son, who had an illusion act himself, all died young but Brodie continued to play the boards in lesser halls until he died on 19 October 1939 shortly after appearing at the Olympia, Blackpool Sands.

In 1975 Dr R.H. Hales escaped from Byeways, Indiana's biggest lunatic asylum, by hiding in a disused refrigerator. Two days later he presented himself before the Appointments Board of Whitehill prison applying for a position of Senior Medical Adviser. He gave a 'brilliant interview' said the Board's Chairman and retained the position until he was recognised when a photograph of him appeared in the local newspaper.

IN JANUARY 2005 Barian Baluchi appeared at Middlesex Crown Court and admitted 30 charges of preparing psychiatric reports on hundreds of asylum seekers. Baluchi, who claimed he had trained at Harvard, Columbia, Newcastle and Sussex universities as well as Leeds Medical School, was in fact an Iranian-born mini-cab driver from south-west London. In the 1990s he bought a PhD from the US and took over the identity of a trainee doctor who had let his provisional registration lapse. Apart from his deception as a psychiatrist he had also undertaken minor operations, charging one patient £150 to remove a wart from his penis. He was jailed for ten years. During his life as a doctor he netted more than £1.5 million.

AT LEAST HE does not seem to have caused as much physical damage as Florida-born Reinaldo Silvestre who posed as a cosmetic surgeon and operated on a former Mr Mexico. With his body-building career on the slide, Alexander Baez went to Silvestre's Ocean Health Center in Miami for pectoral muscle enlargement. When he recovered from the horse-tranquiliser anaesthetic administered by Silvestre, Baez found he had been given female breast implants which began leaking immediately. In 1999 charged with fraud, aggravated battery and practising medicine without a licence, Silvestre absconded his bail and went to Belize where he was found five years later teaching medical students. In March 2006, he received seven and a half years in prison.

IN JANUARY 2006 Daniel Serrano, a Beverly Hills doctor, was jailed for 18 months after pleading guilty to smuggling and the use of unapproved drugs. He had been treating patients with his 'miracle' wrinkle remover. Instead of expensive European silicone injections, he was using industrial grade silicone, which was the equivalent of car oil.

Perhaps the greatest of the medical fraudsters has been Dr Albert Abrams of San Francisco. A genuine doctor, he had studied at Heildelberg and had been chief pathologist of the Cooper Medical Institute. During his career, however, he developed the ERA (Electronic Reactions of Abrams) which spawned a number of machines including the Dynomizer that could diagnose any known disease from a single drop of blood, fresh or old. Unfortunately the machine tended to make cluster diagnoses, warning the patient he had cancer and diabetes as well as syphilis. Naturally, Abrams also had machines such as the Oscilloclast which could usually cure the diseases. In 1921 there were 3,500 doctors using ERA, having trained at $200 a time. Then in 1923 a man diagnosed with terminal cancer was cured by a series of ERA treatments. Cured until he died a month later that is.

Now there were serious questions asked about ERA. On one side was ranged the American Medical Association; on the other, ERA supporters backed by prominent figures such as the authors Upton Sinclair and the gullible, at least in these matters, Sir Arthur Conan Doyle. *Scientific American* gave an ERA doctor six vials to examine and diagnose what they might be. All six findings were wrong but he defended himself by pointing out that the labels were in red ink, which had confused the machine.

The system was further discredited when another practitioner diagnosed a sample as disclosing malaria, cancer, diabetes and syphilis. In fact it had come from a cockerel. His own machines failing to save him, Abrams died of pneumonia in January 1924. After his death one was dismantled and found to contain only a series of wires, lights and buzzers.

A<small>T THE OTHER</small> end of the scale some operators work at a more limited level. One Australian quack physician in the 1920s was Breedan Hames of the Higher Thought Temple of Truth who claimed, 'I am the link between God and Soul' and that through 'Realisation' he could cure cancer and regrow a diseased eye. The Perth scandal sheet *Truth* sent along a woman reporter to investigate, and after paying an entrance fee of a shilling and a further two for a diagnosis she was told she had a growth on her liver. Happily, four 'Realisations' would cure it. She would not feel pain but there would be a smell like burning rubber. *Truth* sent her to a doctor who 'pronounced she was well in every way'. Shortly after that the good Hames was run out of town on a rail, so to speak.

S<small>OME PEOPLE</small> simply cannot stop wanting to be doctors. In the US in May 2004 70-year-old Gerald Barnes started his fifth sentence for impersonating a doctor. He had escaped from a federal prison where he was serving his fourth sentence and resumed his chosen profession. Barnes, born Barnbaum, had adopted the name and credentials of a doctor from Stockton, California.

F<small>REDDRICK MARK</small> Brito posed not only as a psychiatrist but also as a Catholic priest. In his role as a doctor he was appointed to work with the Los Angeles County Public Defender's office, and during his time in Tucson and Phoenix he performed Mass, funerals, weddings and christenings. A man of many talents, shortly after his release from prison for embezzlement he was hired as the executive director of the National Kidney Foundation of Southern California. Although, over time, he has been sentenced to more than 11 years in prison, in

2005 he could be found fundraising on behalf of the San Gabriel Valley Chapter of the American Red Cross.

IN THE EARLY years following the First World War, Dr Macaura produced the Pulsocon, a machine with a mechanical vibrator which could cure almost any ailment known to man. Exposed by the newspapers he decamped to Paris where he was sentenced to three years for practising medicine without a licence. In 1925 he was back in England, this time with the O'Lectron, which 'produces both mechanical and magnetic oscillations' giving 'man control over the circulation of his blood and the atoms of which he is composed'. A real workhorse, the machine stopped pain, joint loosening and 'could overcome paralysis, rheumatism, deafness and obesity'. It also cured gonorrhoea and piles. Until he was exposed by the magazine *John Bull* the altruistic doctor was allowing the public to pay a mere four guineas for the machine, which he said cost 15 guineas to produce.

IN 1916 SERGEANT James Shearer who claimed to have a medical degree from the University of Washington convinced army doctors that Shearer's Delineator would provide immediate help for wounded men. Basically, they had to stand in front of the box which produced what amounted to ticker-tape showing each man's organs. The *British Medical Journal* was among those convinced it could be a major contribution to saving lives and *The Times* thought it 'a remarkable scientific discovery'. Emboldened, Shearer now claimed his box could be extended to military use as an enemy aircraft detector. It seems that doctors had not opened the box, but the Security Services did – and found it contained the mechanism of a pianola, which silently played reels of paper.

JEAN-CLAUDE ROMAND was a man who spent the last 18 years of his life in an extended con trick deceiving his wife, children, mistress, friends and parents.

In 1975 he failed to turn up for his examination as a second-year medical student in Lyon, France, but he appeared to continue his studies. He married Florence Crolet and told her he had passed his final examinations and had become a medical research assistant and then a research scientist with the World Health Organisation in Geneva. Nobody, not even Florence, was given his office telephone number; his work and the meetings he attended were too important to be disturbed. He insisted he could only be contacted by a bleeper and would immediately return the call. He took the children to school each day and then drove on to Geneva where he would go to the WHO, take what leaflets he could and use the banking facilities and post office in the visitors' part of the building. After that he would go to a café or a service station car park and read the material, sleep and have a sandwich. Sometimes, when he said he had to travel on behalf of the WHO, he would go to a hotel in Geneva and stay there for the duration, checking on the weather in the city where he was meant to be before phoning home. Presents were bought in a gift shop.

And how did he finance this deception? First, his wife worked but he claimed that as a highly placed civil servant he could make some high return investments. His parents put their money at his disposal and so did his mistress and her parents and he lived off their capital. In the early 1990s, he falsely claimed he was suffering from cancer and was being treated by a noted oncologist. It all unravelled in 1992, when the headmaster at his children's school, who did not know of Romand's ban on telephone calls, rang the WHO and discovered that he could not be found in the internal directory. He was also running out of capital and his now former mistress was demanding the return of her money.

In the first week of 1993 he decided to kill his family, his mistress and possibly himself. He bought a stun wand, silencer and cartridges for a .22 rifle and two gas canisters. First, he shot his parents and their dog and then used the wand on his one-time mistress. She managed to calm him down and he promised to return her money after the weekend. Instead he went home, killed his wife with blows to the head, shot the children and set fire to the house.

That year he received life imprisonment with no possibility of parole for 22 years.

Madame Rachel

ONE OF THE GREAT English conwomen – blackmailer, abortionist and procurer – of the latter half of the nineteenth century was Sarah Russell, better known as Madame Rachel. In 1862 she opened her Temple of Beauty, of which she was the self-styled priestess, at 47 Bond Street, London. On her way from her East End origins she had married a Philip Levison, kept a fried fish shop, and sold bottles and rabbit skins from a barrow in Wapping. Now, from her Temple she duped middle-aged and fading beauties out of whatever their or their husbands' pockets would stand by selling 'dew from a magnetic rock in the Sahara', which was, in fact, straight from the Thames. To claim the treatments did not work or that Madame had not actually supplied the Morocco Beauty Balm or the Circassian Hair Wash would only court ridicule and the clients paid up.

Then in 1868 she duped the homely 50-year-old widow, Mrs Borrodaile, into believing that the rakish Lord Ranelagh, who had seen her twice, was infatuated with her and wished to marry her. Quite what he was doing at Madame's emporium was never satisfactorily explained. Before she came to her senses Mrs Borrodaile paid over £4,000 to Madame who dictated letters for her to write to the noble Lord (after a glass of whisky, Mrs Borrodaile told the court) offering to darn his socks and buy him a pair of boots. His Lordship's apparently loving replies were dictated by Madame to James Minton, an auctioneer's clerk.

At her trial, Madame's daughter told the court that it would be a breach of professional trust to tell the court the origin of Jordan Water priced at a guinea a bottle. She would, however, say it came from the East. 'Wapping is in the East,' remarked counsel. Madame received a five-year sentence and in 1878 drew the same sentence for another fraud on a young woman. This time she did not survive, dying from dropsy on 12 October 1880 at Knap Hill Prison for Women near Woking. In its list of obituaries for the year the final entry in *The Times* was 'and last, but not least, Madame Rachel'.

All for love

IN 1997 THE 60-year-old balding conman Fred Harris became his sister – Frances Jacqueline – when he set up what he hoped would be a $100 million swindle. He advertised a business for sale, which included as its capital US bearer bonds for 'discounting in the future'. He forged five bearer bonds each with a face value of $20 million and, as Frances, tried to authenticate the forgery. Unfortunately his solicitors contacted the police. At first the police were looking for a brother and sister team and it was not until he was arrested that his identity was discovered. The Hove Crown Court, East Sussex, was told that Harris, who had convictions for deception going back to 1975, had a gender identification problem and that he was halfway through the transformation process. His counsel urged the judge that a long prison sentence was not necessary, adding, 'Consider what shower-time is going to be like for this defendant.' He received three years.

THOSE WHO operate on the edge of the law are often the most vulnerable to the confidence trick. In February 2006 John Quinn was convicted of stealing more than $100,000, over a period of 20 years, from his friend and partner in two illegal brothels in Melbourne. Initially, Quinn told his partner that they were being blackmailed by standover men, or extortionists, with threats to go to the police to reveal all. Flushed with the success of the story, he expanded it over the next two decades inventing corrupt police, estate agents and tax officers, all of whom were supposedly about to blow the whistle. Quinn even told his partner he had gone to a lawyer who advised him that they should pay up. The one time successful businessman eventually filed for bankruptcy. The scam came undone when the man's now adult sons became suspicious and arranged for Quinn to be put under surveillance. In March 2006 he received a four-year sentence.

Possibly the most-married conman has been Giovanni Vigliotto whose real name was probably the less exotic but appropriately sounding Fred Jipp. Vigliotto/Jipp is thought to have married 104 women from eighteen US states and nine countries between 1949 and 1981. Vigliotto, a jeans-and-tennis-shoes-clad flea-market trader, picked women who lived some distance from him and, after persuading them to come to live with him, packed their belongings into a truck and drove off to sell them in the flea markets.

However, the one-hundred-and-fifth victim, 42-year-old Patricia Gardiner who married him in Mesa, Arizona, traced him to a flea market in Florida. On 11 April 1983 Vigliotto was sentenced to 28 years for fraud and six for bigamy by a court in Phoenix.

WOMEN ALSO can be serial seducers. Emma Golightly, from North Tyneside, posing as a wealthy businesswoman used lonely hearts columns to meet wealthy men. She showered them and herself with exotic gifts, all paid for with the men's own credit cards. Within weeks of meeting Golightly, the men invariably agreed to marry her, as she led them to believe she was suffering from terminal cancer. She was jailed for two years in January 2007 after admitting that she conned at least three men out of more than £100,000. She had asked for a further 60 offences of deception to be taken into consideration.

EMMA WAS only treading in the path of 36-year-old Caroline Morgan who at various times claimed she had brain, liver and bowel cancer and took a number of unsuspecting men for £30,000. To help things along, she also had a dead daughter. In fact she had a number of living children, all of whom later met up with an electrician who had married her and had given up his job to care for her.

Her scam came apart when his daughter became suspicious and found that her stepmother's 'morphine' tablets were merely antibiotics. Sentenced to 18 months' imprisonment Morgan was released in July 2006, and in February 2007 was the subject of a BBC television programme in which she claimed she had now been diagnosed as having bipolar disorder.

IN 1746 MARY Hamilton, also known as Charles, George and William Hamilton, married probably for the last time. Mary Price was to be her fourteenth wife. It lasted for three months before neighbours kindly told Mary Price that her husband was not all he seemed to be. Hamilton appeared at Taunton Quarter Sessions and was sentenced to six months together with a whipping in Taunton, Glastonbury,

Wells and Shepton Mallet. She was also ordered to find security for her future good behaviour. Her exploits were the basis for Henry Fielding's novel, *The Female Husband*.

LYING ON A stretcher in 1945, Susanna Mildred Hill from Washington D.C. pleaded guilty to frauds on up to 100 victims. Since the beginning of the decade the 200-pound woman, then in her sixties and the mother of ten children, had run a series of matrimonial and lonely hearts clubs using a picture of the prettiest of her daughters. Who would not want to marry a young girl with substantial savings and with an inheritance around the corner?

Over the years the hapless men sent jewellery and money. Sometimes Miss Hill's 'Mom' was ill and they contributed to medical bills. Hill had several self-imposed rules, one of which was that no applicants within 500 miles of Washington received a reply. If by chance the suitors showed up at her home there was Mrs Hill acting as housekeeper to say the girl was away. If they became too persistent then the correspondence was terminated with a letter saying the worthless child had run off with a salesman; all in all the suitor was better off without her. She received five years.

MILDRED HILL'S victims were very much more fortunate than those of Raymond Fernandez and his partner Martha Beck, who shortly after the Second World War worked a far more lethal version of the Lonely Hearts Game.

Tall and thin and with a neat little wig, the Spanish–American Fernandez targeted women in their fifties and sixties, answering their advertisements and bowling them over with old-world courtesy and the attention he paid them. First there would be a letter from

'Charles Martin' saying he was unmarried, fair looking and 'considered kind' and in perfect health. He had a salary of $85. He enclosed a stamped-addressed envelope. When he actually appeared it was for many women love at first sight. He omitted to tell them of his venereal disease.

Then at Christmas 1947 he answered an advertisement from a young woman in Pensacola, Florida. Instead of the lithe young thing he expected, he met the obese Martha Beck, a 28-year-old matron of a home for crippled children. In turn, he seems to have been bowled over by her and together they set up a business, with Fernandez answering advertisements and then introducing the women to his 'sister' Martha before marrying them and moving on.

Very often they both moved into the homes of the unfortunate women. This they did in January 1949 with 28-year-old Delphine Downing, and Rainelle, her two-year-old daughter, both of whom promptly disappeared. Neighbours went to the police and when they called at Mrs Downing's Grand Rapids home they found her and her daughter buried in the basement. Mrs Downing had been shot and when Rainelle would not stop crying Martha Beck had drowned her. They made a mere $500 from Delphine's death.

When arrested, Fernandez was happy to make a full confession. Even before he met Martha Beck he had been disposing of unwanted women. In early 1947 Lucilla Thompson was taken by him on honeymoon to Spain where she died in a non-existent train crash; in fact, he had poisoned her with digitalis. He moved in with her mother, Pearl Wilson, and cheated her of her money. Another woman, Myrtle Young, had also died from an overdose. In all there were some 17 women who died.

Beck and Fernandez might have received life without parole in Michigan but a Janet Fay, who did not mind being swindled but could not bear Fernandez leaving her, had been strangled with a scarf in New York, which still had the death penalty. The pair were extradited and finally executed on 8 March 1951. Curiously, they did seem to love each other. Martha had been appallingly jealous when Fernandez actually had sex with the women.

Most of Fernandez's addresses came from Mother Dinene's Friendly Club in New York, which was promptly closed by the police. She immediately reopened under another name.

At one time Annie Gleeson, who later toured Europe as the daughter of President Ulysses S. Grant, worked in a panel joint in Chicago. She described it as:

> They literally had sliding panels in the bedrooms, and what you had to do was get the mark's clothes on the sofa near the panel. Out would come his pocketbook and the money in it would be replaced by paper cut into the shape of bank notes. They'd paid in advance so there was no reason for them to reach in until they were well away. I know May Sharpe once or twice worked a version with her maid Skinner hiding under a table but I always reckoned that was too risky. But May was always a chancer, pure if not simple.
>
> Mickey [her husband] and the others would reach in whilst he was otherwise occupied. The best of them was run by Lizzie Davenport at 202 Custom House Place and I worked there a few times.

ONE OF THE stranger murder cases took place in Hammond, Indiana in 1922. Middle-aged Frank McNally had married his house-keeper, the 26-year-old divorcee Hazel. In December 1921 she re-turned from hospital where she had, she said, given birth to twins Frank and Hazel. She claimed that their eyes were too weak to be exposed to direct light and that apart from a brief glimpse all Frank could do was to stand outside the bedroom door and listen to the babies cry. The next month the health of the twins suddenly deteriorated and Hazel took them to a Chicago hospital where they apparently died. Curiously, Hazel persuaded Frank to go along with deceiving the neighbours by pretending that two dolls she had purchased were the babies. Later he would tell the court that when he wanted to stop the deception she hit him, stabbed him and threw an alarm clock at him. She then left McNally and went to live in South Bend, Indiana.

Frank McNally had his suspicions that she had killed the children and went to the police. As a result, in October 1922, Hazel was arrested and charged with murder. However, the evidence was not all that strong: Frank said he had seen her wipe blood from the ear of one of the children, a neighbour said the same about one of the children's nose, a 17-year-old girl said she had carried one of the chil-dren on to the street but could not say if it was alive or dead. Hazel McNally told the police there had never been twins. She had faked the pregnancy because of her husband's constant nagging for her to have children and had purchased two dolls to make the crying noises.

The prosecution claimed it would produce a doctor to say she had been pregnant. The defence said they would produce the doctor who had performed an early hysterectomy on her. The prosecution said they would produce Raymond, her seven-year-old son by a previous marriage. The defence said Raymond was adopted.

When it came to it, the crowded public gallery was sadly disap-pointed. No such evidence was called because the case turned on the fact that the prosecution could not produce the body of either of the twins. The English law of no body, no confession, no case still applied. On 20 October she was acquitted in triumph with the court-room packed with women supporters. When she left after being photographed shaking hands with the judge, she said she would be purchasing two more dolls, divorce McNally and begin to study law. Curiously, it was not the first time she had simulated pregnancy. As a teenager she had convinced her parents and the neighbours she was pregnant, purchasing a doll to bolster her claim.

FRAUDSTERS often want money to help with illness and death, but in 2006 Sarah and Kris Everson tricked their neighbours and work colleagues in Missouri into helping pay for the birth of non-existent sextuplets. In all they raked in $3,500. To help with the deception Ms Everson put on 40 pounds in weight and let everyone know about her pregnancy pains. She bought layettes for six and showed off the nursery ready for the four boys and two girls as soon as they were ready to come home. They each received four years' probation.

ONE OF 'COUNT' Victor Lustig's minor swindles was of girls in brothels. On leaving he would show a $50 bill which he would apparently tuck into their stocking tops telling them that if they looked before the next day it would turn into tissue paper. The girls were naturally unable to stop themselves looking at what, if gen-uine, would have been a handsome fee.

Lustig's scam may have seemed simple but it was still working in a slightly different fashion – and with better rewards – in the late twentieth century. In the 1990s, a swindle was being worked, in theory out of Antwerp but in reality from Florida, selling poor-quality sapphires as guaranteed high-grade stones. Each came in a sealed plastic bubble with a certificate stating that if the original seal was torn or disturbed the guarantee was invalid.

CONS CAN ALSO be perpetrated at long range and over a long time. In 1910 George Osborne suddenly discovered that his fiancée Gladys Wilson of Philadelphia was, in reality, William Barnes, a mechanic. Wilson/Barnes had collected around £1,200 from Osborne over the previous 14 years, during which time Osborne had remained 'faithful to her'. He had always been dissuaded from visiting Philadelphia and had conducted the romance from Southington, Connecticut, where he had a watch-repair business.

MICHAEL KAROLY had at least three lives, beginning in 1920 as Carl Hadju, the son of a tailor in Hungary. By the time he reached England in the 1940s he was Baron Carl Hadju opening an estate agency and raising money for Hungarian freedom fighters who never received it. In 1957 he was exposed by the *Sunday Pictorial* and declared bankrupt, and that was when he became Karoly.

In April 1963 he was bound over to be of good behaviour after being found dressed as a woman in a Hertford hotel on Good Friday. In 1966 his wife, Phyllis, died in Amsterdam and his stepson was killed in a car accident. In May that year he was given four months for obtaining credit as a bankrupt and related offences. He was now claiming to have qualified as a hypnotherapist.

In 1968 he became Dr Charlotte Bach, a widow with a degree in philosophy at Budapest University, a pose he maintained for the rest of his life. As Dr Bach, he wrote a book claiming that transvestites held the key to evolution, a theme that was taken up by the author Colin Wilson. Rather more excitingly, as a sideline he was the dominatrix,

Daphne Lyell-Manson, receiving this testimonial from a satisfied client, 'You were most generous and kind to expend so much energy on my ugly male backside.' He died of cancer, as Dr Bach, in 1981.

IN THE EARLY 1970s, Ron Reed arrived in Toledo, Ohio. For his sins, he went to a fortune-teller, Carolyn Matuszak, telling her he was lonely. She had just the answer for him; she had a beautiful friend, Kyle Stratton, who had, as is usually the case, both advantages and disadvantages. On the plus side she was due to inherit a substantial fortune, on the negative side she was in hospital on a dialysis machine after a car accident. Worse, there was a lawyer in the background who had managed to keep all visitors out of the hospital.

Why didn't Ron write to her? And that was the start of a beautiful friendship; letters were written, photographs exchanged and soon Kyle was making surreptitious phone calls. She also kept in touch with Carolyn who told Ron that the lawyer was holding up Kyle's money so that not only could she not buy herself luxury goods but she was also having a hard time paying for her treatment. Ron took out loans and paid for three operations.

The friendship grew closer. There were daily letters and gifts and, indeed, Kyle started to call herself his wife. Over the years he began to think that if he went out with another girl he was being unfaithful. When he bought himself a new car and tried to cut down on the money he was sending Kyle, Carolyn was incensed on behalf of her friend. How could he think more of a car than her?

This was the moment the worm turned; Ron told a friend of his romance. The friend thought it smelled, and Ron went to the police. What was worse than discovering that Kyle was a figment of Carolyn's imagination was that she had not even been faithful to him. Kyle/Carolyn had been writing to at least 20 other men, all of whom had been sending money, gifts and flowers.

In the end he was quite lucky. Carolyn Matuszak repaid Ron all but $10,000 of his money. Neither he nor the other 'jilted' men wished to prosecute.

PERHAPS EVEN more talented than Carolyn Matuszak was Kirksey McCord Nix Jnr, convicted for the robbery and murder on Easter Sunday 1971 of Frank Corso, a New Orleans grocer. In March 1972 he was found guilty but the jury voted against the death penalty and he received life 'at hard labour'. The sentence meant that he could never be paroled but could only receive a governor's pardon. In a way it was the making of Nix's career.

From inside Angola prison, he began an elaborate scam on homosexuals by setting up what appeared to be a dating agency. In this enterprise, with the assistance of his girlfriend Sheri LaRa Sharpe and a new wife Kellye Dawn Nix whom he purported to marry in prison, he conned around a million dollars from lonely men.

The scheme involved the placing of an advertisement for a 'summer lover' in a local paper. When it was answered, the con involved writing back explaining that the 'lover' Eddie was in some serious, if temporary, difficulties. Could Eddie call collect and explain things? A picture of a handsome young stud was enclosed. The call came through from a rehabilitation programme for first offenders. The victim would speak to a correctional officer who explained that the potential lover was a decent boy at heart. Eventually the victim would put up the air fare for the boy to travel to the potential lover. Then followed a series of disasters – a fight in a lavatory, compensation to avoid a prosecution, dental work, an emergency operation – all of which, to keep Eddie out of prison and to get him nearer the victim, required more and more money to be sent. The writer James Dickey lost $17,000 in this way.

What was amazing was that all the parts – Eddie, the correctional officer, policemen and social workers – were played by Nix. And, with variations and refinements, it was successfully repeated time and again. Apart from purchasing privileges in Angola, which Nix said cost him $12,000 a month, the bulk of the money was used to try to obtain parole. As for complaints by the victims, the police were not all that interested in the misfortunes of elderly chicken-hawkers looking for young lovers. Even had they been, the complicated telephone system in Angola would almost certainly have thwarted their efforts to find out which of the prisoners had been operating the con.

In 1990 at the age of 26, Charles Daugherty, a black man, was arrested for criminal impersonation when he enrolled at Coronado High School, Colorado Springs as a 17-year-old white female student and joined the all-female cheerleading squad. For this he was placed on probation. Four years later, as Storme Aerison, he posed as a supermodel who, by using heavy make-up and coloured contact lenses, appeared to be a white woman with long, platinum-blond hair and blue eyes. Daugherty claimed to be producing a calendar with himself, as Storme, appearing on all the pages. He built up an entourage of photographers and other supporters who were to be paid after production. There were allegations that he also defrauded calendar companies and overseas hotels out of money, airline tickets and rooms by promising to advertise their businesses in the calendar. Given bail he moved to Hawaii and in early 2007 after long legal wrangling and a period of time in a mental hospital, he was found fit to stand trial. The trial has yet to be heard. He has pleaded not guilty.

'Dapper Dan' Collins

'COUNT' VICTOR LUSTIG'S long-time helpmate, 'Dapper' Dan Collins, will repay more study than has so far been accorded him. Not too many fraudsmen spice their careers with murder, but Collins was involved in at least three investigations. The first time was over the 1920 murder, in New York, of fading playboy Joseph Elwell. In May the next year he was questioned over the shooting of manufacturer John H. Reid in New York in what was thought to be an affair of the heart. Finally he was interviewed over the murder of silent-film director William Desmond Taylor in Hollywood in February 1922. In none of the investigations was he charged.

Born Robert Arthur Tourbillon in Atlanta, Georgia, in 1880, he first worked in a circus riding a bicycle in a cage full of lions – they were doped. He came to New York at the turn of the century, and with his undoubted charm it was easy for him to fleece women.

DAPPER DAN COLLINS

Apart from working with Lustig – he was often his secretary, and at a crucial moment would call the Count away to the telephone leaving the suckers in an empty room – he was also a leader in his own right and perfected a little wrinkle on the Badger Game.

In his version it was he who was the apparent victim and not the woman whom he had selected to pay for his next suit of clothes. However, once in the room, seemingly the 'police' directed their attention more to him than to the woman, claiming that he had transported a woman across a state line to commit a felony. This was in breach of the so-called Mann Act which, although intended to stamp out prostitution, was regularly used against adulterous couples including Charlie Chaplin and the architect Frank Lloyd Wright. To protect the woman – always upper class and married – from what would be social humiliation, Collins was the one who initially handed over his wallet to avoid arrest and prosecution. The problem was that there was insufficient in it to meet the 'police' demands. The woman could be relied on to ante-up her furs, jewellery and cash.

During Prohibition, Collins had his yacht raided and a woman from Connecticut handed over diamonds and furs worth $7,000 to avoid the appalling publicity which would accompany his prosecution. At the time he was also transporting illegal immigrants on the yacht and 'police' now took all their possessions in addition to the $1,000 fare each had paid Collins.

In 1924 he went to Europe to avoid arrest in New York. He was, however, recognised by a New York police officer who had been sent to arrest another suspect and was extradited on the SS *Paris*. Back in the US he was acquitted but then returned to Europe once more to help Lustig sell the Eiffel Tower. Then, again with the Count, he became a supplier of liquor to the speakeasies owned by the gangster Jack 'Legs' Diamond. Just as Lustig had cheated Capone so, by switching labels, they cheated Diamond and were fortunate to be able to leave the country before he was able to take reprisals when he discovered the scam. Matters calmed down; Collins reappeared and in 1929 was sentenced to five years over a swindle in which a New Jersey farmer was relieved of $30,000. On his release he announced he had retired and was now to lead a sedentary life.

However, the police had no doubt who helped in Lustig's escape from the Manhattan detention centre on 25 August 1935; within a matter of hours they had collected Collins from the nearby Hotel Belvedere. What they wished to learn was the real name of the woman – of whom there was now no sign – who had for the past month been visiting Lustig. Collins remained silent and served six months for contempt and for his pains.

After Lustig's recapture in Pittsburgh and his subsequent imprisonment, the police believed, probably incorrectly, that Collins knew where his former partner had hidden much of his forged currency (Lustig had taken up counterfeiting after he gave up the Money Box Game) and he was kept under surveillance. If he did know where the money was stashed he never revealed it. But there was a nasty scrape when, in September 1936, he and four others were arrested under the 1934 Gold Reserve Act in a gold-selling swindle. It was the usual scam: the mark was sold the gold and then fake policemen moved in to arrest everyone with the result that the mark was out both of his money and the gold. However, one of those involved was B.E. Leibman – an FBI agent – who had infiltrated the group looking for the forged money and who had been playing along in the scam. Fortunately, for most concerned, the prosecution's evidence was hopelessly contaminated and, after a week in custody, the charges against Collins were dismissed.

In June 1939 Collins appeared before the courts for the last time. He had been posing as an immigration officer extorting $200 from Helen Modzelewski, the wife of an illegal Jewish immigrant. Unfortunately he went back for more and this time she called the police. On his arrest he was described as, once again, being his usual dapper self with the neat grey spats he always wore and a stylish grey hat over his now iron-grey hair. However, when he appeared for sentencing he was nearly 60 and was showing his age. As a fourth-time offender he was entitled to expect a lengthy sentence and, despite the relatively little money he had obtained on this occasion, he received one of 15 to 30 years. 'I've been around but today I'm just an old reprobate,' he told reporters before his sentence, and afterwards remarked, 'The only way I'll ever come out again is feet first.'

He was right. He died in Attica prison in upstate New York in 1951. No one attended his burial service.

Monumental frauds

'COUNT' VICTOR LUSTIG'S most outrageous scam took place in Paris in 1925. Working with 'Dapper' Dan Collins, Lustig took bids for the sale of the Eiffel Tower as scrap. Posing as the deputy general of the Ministry of Posts and Telegraphs, he sold it for an estimated $50,000 to an André Poisson who thought the deal would establish him in the big time. Lustig and Collins went off to Vienna but when they found Poisson had not been to the police they returned and sold the tower a second time for $75,000. This time, however, the mark did inform the police and the 'Count' hurriedly absented himself from Europe and set up home in the US with the proceeds.

LUSTIG MAY have sold the Eiffel Tower twice, but in a five-week period in the 1920s it is said that a Scots-born actor, Arthur Furguson, managed to sell Nelson's Column to an American tourist for a modest £6,000, telling him that the statue was being pulled down and sold to help repay the National Debt. He also sold Big Ben for a £1,000 and took a deposit of £2,000 for the sale of Buckingham Palace. He had apparently had the idea when taking the part of a duped American in a play in Manchester. In around 1925 he travelled to the US where he leased out the White House for 99 years for the

sum of $100,000. His downfall came when he tried to sell the Statue of Liberty to an Australian. He received five years and was released in 1930. Undaunted he continued his life as a conman, this time in California, until his death in 1938.

THE FIRST record of anyone being convicted for selling the Brooklyn Bridge came in 1901, 20 years after it was built. Then William Mc-Cloundy was sentenced to two and a half years in Sing Sing. In 1911 he went to prison for selling lots in City Hall Park and other property owned by the city of New York. In July 1928, then aged 68, he was arrested for selling lots on Highland Boulevard, Brooklyn.

However, the man who most regularly sold the bridge was George C. Parker who also disposed of Grant's Tomb, the Museum of Modern Art, the original Madison Square Garden and the Statue of Liberty. The going rate could be from as little as $50 up to whatever he thought the sucker would pay. On other occasions Parker would accept deposits. At its simplest level he told the mark that he owned the bridge and offered the man a job operating a toll gate which was to charge a penny a crossing. The man would suggest that a higher rate could be obtained, and when Parker seemed dubious, would offer to buy the bridge itself. From time to time police would have to remove purchasers who were actually trying to erect toll barriers. He served short sentences until he was finally sentenced to life imprisonment by Judge McLaughlin in Kings County Court on 17 December 1928 and died in Sing Sing in 1937.

The sale of Brooklyn Bridge was standard fare for the conman of the early twentieth century; Reed Waddell, the 'Yellow Kid' Weill and the Gondorf Brothers are among those said to have been involved. Eventually the authorities took to issuing leaflets telling immigrants at Ellis Island that public buildings were not for sale.

It was not, however, always immigrants who were duped. In September 1914 it was reported that a St Louis man had bought a bridge across the Mississippi.

THE YEAR AFTER Parker and McCloundy went down, two swindlers sold the information booth at New York's Grand Central Station to two Italian fruiterers, Tony and Nick Fortunato for $100,000. As Wilson A. Blodgett and T. Remington Grenfell, President and Vice President of the Grand Central Holding Corporation, they told the brothers that in future all queries which had previously been answered by attendants at the booth would be dealt with by the ticket salesmen. Now the way was clear for a fruit-stand concession and who better than the brothers to run it? The papers were signed allowing the brothers to take over at 9.00 a.m. precisely on 1 April 1929.

When the day came the unfortunate pair, who had hired carpenters, found the booth occupied and ordered the clerks out. When they were told they had been swindled they blamed the railroad company itself as perpetrating the fraud and, for some years, they would go to Grand Central Station threatening and abusing the staff at the booth. The fraudsters were never identified.

SOMETIMES potential victims fight back. In 2005 an Internet scammer using the pseudonym 'Genevieve' tried to obtain money from 'Vidocq' to help launder the ill-gotten gains from a coup in Liberia.

The tables were turned because, after a prolonged exchange of emails, Vidocq instead offered Genevieve shares in the Brooklyn Bridge. Genevieve should have known better. Vidocq was the name of a nineteenth-century French thief turned detective who became the first head of the Sûrété.

In 1961 the Ceylonese conman, Charles Da Silva, is credited with selling a Grimsby fishing fleet, sight unseen, to a farmer whom he met in the first-class breakfast compartment on the Hull to Kings Cross train. The non-existent trawlers were meant to be coming from Sweden and going to Ceylon. The farmer had money from a syndicate to buy meat in Smithfield market and, according to underworld legend, by the time the train pulled into the platform Charles had the money. In fact, the scam was actually worked over several meetings in a Kensington hotel.

There was outrage in 1998 and again in 2004 when Italian government ministers suggested that the Colosseum in Rome should be sold or leased to private individuals as a way of raising money to reduce Italy's huge budget deficit. Not perhaps such a new idea though; there is a story that as recently as 1966 a West German leased it for ten years at twenty million lire a year, cash in advance, to an American tourist who thought the top level could be converted into a restaurant with a wonderful view over the city.

Michael Dennis Corrigan and Charles Da Silva

ONE OF BRITAIN'S most successful conmen, Michael Dennis Corrigan, committed suicide by strangling himself with his own tie, in Brixton prison on 16 October 1946. Appropriately, he had been reading Christopher Hale's recently published thriller, *Hangman's Tie*.

He often claimed to be an American and sometimes he was Kittery Edward Cassidy, a Canadian whose father had been a Chief Inspector in the Mounties. In fact he was illegitimate and born in Ireland.

In 1915 he was a ship's steward and by the mid 1920s he had a conviction for fraud in Brussels. In 1927 he was acquitted in the UK of failing to register under the Aliens Act. In 1930 he was posing as the President of the Standard Oil Company of the US for which he received five years' penal servitude on 9 September 1930. The year before, he had gone bankrupt in the UK with debts of £108,882 and assets of £30. He had previously been made bankrupt in 1923 but had eventually obtained his discharge. At one time he owned 27 racehorses, running them mainly in Belgium, but was warned-off. In 1937 he was fined for helping smuggle a Frenchman into Britain, and the next year was again fined for making a false declaration to Customs officials. In 1938 as a representative of the Chinese government, he conned a director of a Paris arms firm out of £7,250 for which he received two years. It was then he was described as 'a menace to society' and a 'most plausible swindler and adventurer'.

During the civil war in Spain he got in touch with a number of wealthy men known to be friendly towards Franco and told them that despite the British government's ban he was in a position to sell 24 Hawker warplanes for £200,000. Delegates were taken by

Corrigan to see the planes that he had had parked in rows at Northolt airfield. A lucky one or two were even allowed a close inspection before the money was handed over. The men never received the planes, nor did they take action to retrieve their £200,000.

A short thick-set, bullnecked man who bubbled over with enthusiasm, Corrigan could, said Arthur Thorp the detective who finally arrested him, 'sell dead horses to mounted policemen'. At one time he posed as a general in the Mexican army. 'Anyone with two hundred men under him was a general', he told the court in 1930. Later he was another General, this time in the Chinese army, and over the years worked in the Secret Service, was a Vice-Admiral in the Royal Navy, Commissar for Trade in Britain for the Soviet Union and a representative of the Romanian government placing contracts with British firms. He was due to appear at the Old Bailey charged with posing as acting for a Guatemalan millionaire who, in a scheme involving concessions from the Guatemalan government, would earn millions supplying wood for building aircraft. He had obtained £2,000 from a Wimpole Street dentist as part finance for the scheme. Corrigan also claimed he was buying No. 145 Piccadilly, which had been the home of George VI before his accession.

A good host, thoroughly gregarious, friend of actors, the aristocracy and particularly actresses, it was his boast, 'Everyone knows Micky Corrigan.' He married in 1916 and when in 1928 a photograph was published of Corrigan at the races with the actress Muriel Harrold with a caption that he was engaged to her, his wife sued, obtaining £500 from the *Daily Mirror* for libel. At the same time a Miss Webb was suing him for breach of promise. He then took Miss Harrold's mother for several thousand in a share swindle.

At the time of his arrest he was living in a 17-guineas-a-week Mayfair flat, employing a butler and a personal taxi driver at £25 a week. When he died he left a note for his solicitor saying, 'I deserve everything for being such a greedy fool … I don't think I can face this sentence.'

Another of the best conman of recent years in England, the enormously handsome and good-natured Ceylon-born Charles Da Silva, also committed suicide. It was said of him that he could have been Omar Sharif's better-looking brother. He could pose as an Arab prince and frequently did so. He arrived in England in 1947 and from then on worked both long and short cons. He first fell foul of the courts in 1951 when he was prosecuted over the sale of nylon stockings (then a rare post-war commodity) to Selfridges.

He was also involved with the Soho figures Billy Hill and Albert Dimes and a Mayfair solicitor over a fraud, supposedly selling chinchillas. Da Silva told the punters there were to be chinchilla farms in Ceylon. The solicitor was acquitted and Hill and Dimes were only mentioned in the case, but Da Silva received six years.

One long con of Da Silva's that did not require much in the way of equipment, simply a rudimentary office, was a syndicate he established in 1961 to buy and then sell arms to the Falangists to overthrow the Franco government in Spain. Shares in it were £20,000 or £30,000 a time, depending on how much profit the dupe thought he could make. But Da Silva was regarded as being able to work a short con just as well.

Two stories illustrate both his humour and talent. Wishing to impress a potential mark he had them both invited to 10 Downing Street when Harold Macmillan was Prime Minister. Da Silva had been on a charity committee run by Lady Macmillan and he went over to the Prime Minster, put his hand on his shoulder and whispered something in his ear. Recounting the story Da Silva used to say that the punter was really impressed, but all he'd been saying to Macmillan was, 'Thank you for inviting me.'

Another con that earned him high marks was when he found an American who liked schoolgirls. Da Silva rented a gaggle of prostitutes to dress up, told the American they were from a convent and charged him £25,000 for the name and address of the mother superior.

Unfortunately, for much of his working life he was under the influence of Charles Mitchell, one of the Krays' henchmen, who took 75 per cent of his earnings and of whom he was mortally afraid. For a time the twins protected Da Silva from Mitchell, but when they were convicted in 1969, Mitchell, who had turned Queen's evidence against them and had himself been acquitted, regained his influence over Da Silva. What was left of his earnings, Da Silva frittered away in gaming clubs; he was an inveterate gambler.

He died in a hotel when he was awaiting trial at the Old Bailey for another fraud. The official verdict was suicide but some people, including the crime writer Derek Raymond who for a time acted as his chauffeur, suggested that he was killed to prevent him talking to the police. If this is correct it would not be the first time such a thing has happened. In support of Raymond's theory, Da Silva was a devout member of the Catholic Church, who used to go to Mass in Mayfair every Sunday when he was out of prison and not working.

Law in action

SOME CONMEN are simply unlucky. In 1900 Harry Beale Tress who had been working as a clerk for Robert Edridge, a London solicitor based in Holloway, took over his practice and identity when he died. That year he was successful in a claim for a breach of promise action but pocketed the £25 damages awarded to an Annie Taylor and disappeared. Quite by chance she saw him at a Salvation Army meeting but he escaped and, after working in the print industry for a while, went to Sunderland in December 1905 where he applied for a job as a solicitor's clerk. Unfortunately he applied to the solicitor who had acted against Miss Taylor in the breach of promise action. He received six months.

ON ONE OCCASION during a trial recess, the dishonest New York lawyer Bill Fallon had the prosecutor summoned to the telephone where a female voice informed him of his wife's infidelity. The prosecutor had taken his briefcase with him and, stunned by the news, he left the case and with it the court papers, in the kiosk. When he remembered it he discovered the briefcase had disappeared. Fallon demanded the trial be continued and, without the stolen evidence, he won an acquittal.

The great nineteenth-century New York lawyer Bill Howe had a repertoire of jury tricks, such as digging his nails into female clients' ears to make them scream at appropriate moments. Fallon extended the range, sometimes almost legitimately. On one occasion, in the early 1920s, when defending a Russian for arson and attempted fraud on insurance companies, much of the case depended on discrediting the evidence of a fire officer who said he had smelled kerosene on wet rags. Fallon produced a number of bottles and asked the witness to sniff them in turn and say which contained water and which kerosene. When the man said all five were kerosene, Fallon drank from the fifth bottle saying that, to him, it seemed like water and the jurors should take the bottle into the jury room and taste it for themselves. If it tasted of kerosene then they should convict, if it tasted of water they should acquit. They acquitted. The fireman, after sniffing kerosene from four bottles, still had the fumes in his nostrils when he sniffed the water in the fifth.

In 1923 Fallon was in serious trouble over a charge that he had bribed a juror. More dangerously, he had also fallen foul of William Randolph Hearst and the newspaper tycoon's New York *American*. The allegation was that he had bribed a juror in a stock-market swindle case. He had offered the man $5,000, half down but, true to form, had retained the second half after the acquittal.

Fallon's defence was an all-out attack on Hearst whom he maintained was persecuting him for discovering, in Mexico, birth certificates showing the magnate had fathered twins by his long-time actress companion Marian Davies. On the witness stand he patted his breast pocket to indicate that he had them on him, ready to produce if required. Efforts by the prosecutor to suppress the references were overruled and he certainly was not going to take the chance of having the certificates produced. The damage had been done: including a time-out for dinner, the jury acquitted Fallon in under five hours. He is said to have thanked the jury individually and then turned to Hearst's reporter, Nat Ferber, who had been instrumental in providing the case against him, saying, 'Nat, I promise you I'll never bribe another juror.' Years later Fallon admitted there were no certificates.

GASTON MEANS was regarded by William Burns, the detective who became head of the FBI, as 'the greatest natural detective ever known'. Others saw this one-time towel salesman and lawyer as swindler, blackmailer and murderer. Born in North Carolina in 1880, he joined the Burns Detective Agency, then rivals to the Pinkertons. He left in 1915 to become the personal bodyguard to the eccentric heiress Maude R. King who used to amuse herself by dropping stink bombs in the House of Lords and wine bottles from the Eiffel Tower.

Means saved her from a fake mugging and within two years had separated her from $15,000 before he took her on a hunting trip. The pair became distanced from the other hunters and after a shot was heard he stumbled out of the woods saying, 'Poor Mrs King.' He had, he said, put his .25 Colt revolver in the crotch of a tree while he went to get a drink and she had somehow managed to shoot herself behind the left ear. Charged with murder, Means was acquitted by a jury composed largely of Ku Klux Klanners.

After the First World War he joined the FBI but was indicted in a bootlegging swindle pretending he was collecting graft for the Secretary of State, Andrew Mellon. He was also blackmailing President Harding, threatening to reveal that he was the father of a child by the undistinguished Ohian poetess, Nan Britton.

His final coup came when he told another heiress Mrs Evalyn Walsh McLean that through his underworld contacts he could recover the Lindbergh baby, which had been kidnapped in 1932, taking $104,000 from her in fees and expenses. Charged with false pretences, Means claimed that he had given the money to some lawyers. He received 15 years.

He died in 1939 in the prison hospital at Leavenworth following a heart attack. FBI agents were sent to his bedside to ask him to disclose the whereabouts of the money but, at least so the story goes, he simply smiled and died.

ONE OF THE more dapper and able barristers around the Old Bailey in the late 1960s was Ronald Shulman. Married to one of the daughters of the property magnate, Harold Samuels, he had been involved in what would in the language of the times be described as 'an extremely messy divorce'. A slight man with dark wavy hair and a taste for facetious jokes, he could be seen of an evening in fashionable nightclubs. Shulman was a close friend of the property millionaire Clive Raphael who was killed on 6 March 1970 when his aeroplane, a twin-engined Beagle, plunged into a field in central France killing him, his parents and a woman friend. Shulman's sadness at his friend's death must have been mitigated by the fact that Raphael left him his fortune in a will made two days before his death. His widow, the 21-year-old model Penny Brahms, received only a shilling (or 5p in today's money) together with four photographs of herself in the nude. The shilling was because of Raphael's nickname for her. Her enthusiasm for the will was in direct inverse proportion to the joy Shulman must have felt at his good luck.

Of course, it wasn't luck unless you believe in the phrase that you make your own. The will was a forgery, the result of a conspiracy between Shulman, his one-time mistress and 51-year-old Eric Henry-Alba-Teran, the Duc d'Antin. There were arrests all round but Shulman failed to appear at the committal proceedings and fled the country, alleging that he had received death threats. He was thought to have gone to Brazil, setting a precedent for the Great Train Robber, Ronnie Biggs, for at the time the extradition treaty with that country had lapsed.

At the trial, Peter Bardon, of the Department of Trade and Industry, told the court that he had been called in to assist the French authorities' inquiry as to whether the plane had been deliberately blown up. Shulman, when questioned during the investigation, had asked him whether there was any evidence of sabotage and when he said there was not, 'Shulman seemed surprised.'

In fact, it seems not, as many thought, that Shulman had somehow managed to destroy the aeroplane but that he had taken advantage of the accident by immediately producing the will of a man whom he knew not to have made one.

The girl's counsel said, in the rhetoric of the time, that Shulman had 'sold his soul to the devil'. Her part in the conspiracy had been secured by threats of violence and she had typed out the will with one finger after Shulman had threatened to smash her head against the wall and kill her if she made a mistake.

She was given a suspended sentence by the kindly Common

Serjeant, Mervyn Griffiths-Jones, who accepted she had been under Shulman's domination. 'If you take my advice you will see no more of this other man and forget this now. You are still young. Go back to your family and start again.' The rather older Duc d'Antin could not urge that he had been dominated by Shulman in quite the same way and he received three years' imprisonment to which was added another 12 months for appropriating Raphael's white Rolls-Royce. He was recommended for deportation after he had served his sentence.

From time to time there were sightings of the errant Shulman in Brazil and he was credited, *in absentia*, with the 'Shulman defence' to cocaine smuggling. At Lewes Crown Court, counsel joked among themselves that so many defendants from South America were claiming that they thought the drugs they were found to be smuggling were emeralds, it seemed likely they had been receiving expert English legal advice.

For all that is known Shulman is still living in Brazil.

GIVEN THE general dislike in which lawyers are held worldwide, it is difficult to see why anyone would wish to pose as one. However, in October 2003 Paul Bint, a conman with 24 known aliases, began a four-year and four-month sentence for conning a doctor into believing he was Orlando Pownall who had prosecuted in the Jill Dando murder trial. It was not the first time Bint had been a barrister. In 2000 he had posed as Lachlan Campbell-Brierdon QC, involved in the Lockerbie bombing trial. Once, to help things out, he had stolen a barrister's robes and wig from Birmingham Crown Court. He has also regularly been a doctor and, fascinated by expensive cars, posed as the Duke of Arundel to obtain a test drive in a Maserati. He became a relative of the Lord Chancellor to obtain a Golf GTI Cabriolet.

In the 2003 case he told a hospital consultant that he had crashed his car and lived in The Bishop's Avenue, one of the most expensive streets in Hampstead. She had allowed him to stay in her house and he had walked off with a small amount of cash and a credit card.

After that, he used one stolen from an elderly hospital patient to take out the man's daughter. The court was told that Bint had committed up to 500 crimes in the previous 25 years. He had earlier been released from a 33-month sentence in Scotland where he had posed as a businessman and made off with a £52,000 Aston Martin.

Carrie Morse and Sophie Lyons

MOST WOMEN confidence tricksters set their sights on men, but Carrie Morse was an exception. Born Marion Grass in New Brunswick, Canada, she first appeared in court in 1870 as Marion Warren. In 1875 she tried to borrow against a forged railroad stock certificate, jumped bail and fled to St John's. In 1880 she opened a brokerage house as Marion E. Warren from which she made around $40,000. She went down in Philadelphia after opening an investment business offering ladies a complete guarantee of their money in return for half their profits. Released on a technicality, she married Royal La Touche and then, on his conviction for bigamy, James McDonald. In 1883 she was Carrie Morse, the name by which she was best known, and received two years but was soon back in business as Mme Marion La Touche offering a guarantee for any investment over $300. Arrested, she was again acquitted on a technicality.

She then recruited the bank robber and confidence trickster Sophie Lyons who, as Mrs Cecilia Rigsby, became president of the Women's Banking and Investment Company, which they set up together on 23 West Street, New York. Again only women were allowed to invest their hard-earned savings and the scam, for which neither was arrested, is said to have netted Morse $50,000.

In *Our Rival the Rascal*, written in 1896, two former detectives admitted they had no idea under which name or where Carrie Morse was then working. But working she certainly would have been.

Born Sophie Elkins, the daughter of Sophie Elkins Snr, herself a shoplifter, and a brutal housebreaker father who burned her arms, Sophie Lyons could turn her hand to most things – pickpocketing, shoplifting, confidence tricks and prison escapes on behalf of her husband Ned Lyons whom she once rescued in a snowstorm.

In the late 1870s, she went to Boston where she worked the Badger Game with Kate Leary from New York. It was here they became involved in the celebrated Room Eleven, Revere House case when they stripped a prominent Boston merchant and retained his clothing until he paid $10,000. Not enough funds were available to meet his cheque for when Sophie presented it at the bank. Unwisely she told the clerk where to find the drawer of the cheque and both she and Kate Leary were arrested. The man, whose family life was now in ruins, declining further exposure, refused to appear at court and the pair were discharged.

Moving on to Detroit, she continued working the Badger Game for the next three years. There she met her match; for some weeks she would go each day to the home of a well-known businessman and sit on the horse block outside his house. He retaliated by turning a hose on her and beating a theatrical agent who came to her rescue.

She then went to New York and, after the collapse of Carrie Morse's bank, she fled to Europe where she teamed up with an Englishwoman, Helen Gardner, who posed as the widow of a recently deceased fashionable doctor Edward Temple. When the man's widow went to Egypt, Helen went to Nice and sold options on the late doctor's practice; she later served a sentence in France.

Sophie Lyons went to England where she worked for some years and served a number of sentences before, she claimed, she 'saw the Light'. In 1906 she became the social correspondent for the New York *World* and then, in 1913, she wrote her bestselling autobiography *Why Crime Does Not Pay*. Apart from a few cautionary lines at the end of each chapter, the real intention was to show exactly what fun crime was and how it did pay.

She died in 1926 in Detroit after a robbery at a restaurant where she took her meals. She left her considerable wealth to establish a home for the children of imprisoned criminals, but it was all frittered away in a series of law suits.

Where there's a will ...

AT THE END OF the nineteenth century, one of the more outrageous frauds was attempted by the Liverpool solicitor John Hollis Yates. It concerned the estate of Helen Sherridan who had come from the west of Ireland and married a young officer, Blake, who was stationed in Dublin. Her husband subsequently attained the rank of Lieutenant General and died in 1850. She died in 1883 intestate and consequently, unless heirs could be found, the then considerable fortune of £200,000 would be forfeit to the Crown. The wrangle over the estate continued for over a decade. Yates found a family of the same name in Liverpool and came to a profit-sharing arrangement. If he could establish their claim they would pay him a percentage of the estate.

He went to Ireland where he interviewed many of the 'oldest inhabitants' and sent their statements to counsel to ask what further evidence was required. Advised that birth and marriage certificates were almost essential, he accepted that these would be extremely difficult to forge and as an alternative set about preparing a family bible. He found one of the correct age and began the entries, including a note purporting to be by Martin Sherridan's daughter reading, 'My daughter Helen has run away with a young officer staying in Dublin Castle and has married him privately in Scotland.' It also recorded the death of old Martin Sherridan and the births of the Liverpool Sherridans. Next he had coffin plates prepared and a drawing of a tombstone to bolster the claim.

But his final coup was his undoing. He purchased a silver watch and wanted it engraved 'from Helen Blake to her dear nephew Patrick Sherridan, 1886'. Now, Helen had died in 1883 not 1886 and so had everything gone to plan Yates would have been found out anyway. However, the engraver assumed that Yates wanted the date to be 1896 – why would he want to get a watch engraved with a message from ten years previously? When Yates took the watch back to be altered, the engraver, now suspicious, contacted the police. A warrant to search Yates's offices uncovered the family bible and the watch as well as the coffin plates. Unfortunately he had used a Protestant bible, an unlikely possession for a poor Catholic family in the first half of the nineteenth century. He was sentenced to penal servitude for life in 1896.

I<small>T IS NOT</small> generally accepted that the son of the aviator Charles Lindbergh survived the 1932 kidnapping and murder attributed to Bruno Hauptman, but even in the twenty-first century there are still claimants to the Lindbergh millions.

During the evening of 1 March 1932, Charles, the 19-month-old son of Charles Augustus Lindbergh, who piloted the first non-stop flight alone from New York to Paris in 1927, was kidnapped from his bedroom on the family estate near Hopewell, New Jersey. On 12 May 1932 the decomposed body of a baby was found four miles away and was identified by Charles's mother and a maid.

Nevertheless, in 2002, the count of hopefuls was at least seven. They included Kenneth Kerwin, a factory worker, who claimed that he was the kidnapped baby and could describe in some detail the nursery from which the boy was snatched. Unfortunately his hair and eyes were the wrong colour. Another claimant managed to pass a lie-detector test, while a third and probably the best known has been Harold Olson, a Connecticut businessman who maintains that he, as baby Charles, was kidnapped in connection with a scheme to spring Al Capone from prison. When this failed the gang kindly placed him with foster parents. The most unlikely was a black woman from Oklahoma who spoke of a sex change and skin dye.

ONE OF THE longest surviving cons has involved the so-called Drake fortune. Beginning within a matter of months of the death of Sir Francis Drake on 28 January 1596 it has run, on and off, ever since. Basically the story goes that Drake left a staggering personal fortune from looting Spanish ships on behalf of Queen Elizabeth I and also an illegitimate child from his union with the Queen. If your name was Drake, and even if it was not, could you be that illegitimate child's lawful descendant? Money was needed to finance a suit to release the accumulated billions being held by the British government. There was an outbreak of the scam in the US in the 1830s and another in the 1880s. Then in the twentieth century came one of the greatest exponents of the scheme, Oscar Hartzell from Madison County, Iowa. The story is that his mother had been a victim of the scam, being worked in 1917 by Sudie Whitaker and Milo F. Lewis. He did his research, traced Whitaker and Lewis, retrieved his mother's money and then teamed up with them. Now the Sir Francis Drake Association was born.

With Whitaker and Lewis, Hartzell sold worthless shares in the Drake Inheritance throughout the Midwest, recruiting more and more salesmen. He was undoubtedly a stunning salesman himself. At a single meeting in Quincy, Illinois he signed up almost every adult in town.

Five years on in 1922, so the story goes, he decided to go to England to free the inheritance cached by the rascally British government. In fact his alien's card at the National Archives shows he and others had first been in Britain in 1916, which casts doubt on the story of the swindle of his mother. Investors were sworn to secrecy and silence, and off Hartzell went to London posing as a Texas oil millionaire. Within a matter of months he was the Premier Duke of Buckland receiving and spending $2,500 a week from the US, which had been gathered by an increasing number of agents who peddled the scheme to the gullible and greedy.

In 1927 he cabled back home, 'Settlement delayed for a month. Estate will be handed over with as much speed as His Majesty can conveniently allow.' The next year the Lord Chancellor was ill and could not sign the necessary papers. Then came the Wall Street Crash; it might take him years to free the money; Britain would go bankrupt; negotiations were continuing; President Roosevelt was meeting his advisers every weekend to discuss and insist on payment. The money kept pouring in from the punters and now Hartzell was Baron Hartzell. He was deported from England in February 1933 as an undesirable alien and was promptly arrested in Sioux City, Iowa. Bailed, he still collected more and more investments and even after he was sent to Leavenworth to serve ten years the scam went on until it was finally broken in 1935 with the arrest of the principal agents.

Over the years Hartzell became delusional, seeming actually to believe in his claims. He died at the Medical Centre for Federal Prisoners in Springfield, Missouri on 27 August 1943. It is estimated that the scam had no less than 70,000 victims.

Apart from Hartzell and his agents, the only person to recoup any money from his scam was a London conwoman, Miss St John Montague who worked as a fortune teller in South Kensington. She also employed a shady private detective, Tom Barnard, who plied Hartzell with drink and discovered not only details of his scheme but also that he had managed to impregnate a barmaid during his time in London. As a result, Miss St John Montague blackmailed Hartzell to the tune of some $50,000 over a five-year period.

The Baker Estate Swindle is perhaps not as well known as the Drake Inheritance but between the 1860s and the 1930s it supported up to 40 separate groups of confidence tricksters. The principle was the same as the Drake Inheritance scam. Colonel Jacob Baker died in 1839 and his heirs were entitled to a share in his estate which included thousands of acres of prime land including the whole of downtown Philadelphia. Initially those entitled to shares had to be named Baker but, as the scam went on, Beckers and Barkers were generously included. The scheme was broken up with arrests in the 1930s, and in 1936 one of the ringleaders, 70-year-old lawyer William Cameron Morrow Smith, who over the years had made millions out of the swindle, was jailed. He died a week into his sentence.

The punters did at least get an annual fête for investing in the Edwards Heirs Association. Their annual subscription of $26 was to help the family in its legal battle to gain hold of the estate of Robert Edwards who owned 65 acres of Manhattan Island. The scam was devised in 1880 by the self-styled Dr Herbert E. Edwards and, like the Drake and Baker Inheritance Swindles, ran until the Post Office Department stamped on the organisers in the 1930s.

Aɴʏ ɢᴏᴏᴅ conman will make the best of what often may be limited circumstances. In the late 1890s Sheffield's Albert Marson, known locally as 'The Pitsmoor Millionaire', borrowed money from cycle manufacturer Thomas Eastwood on the basis of him being the heir to gold and vast estates in Canada. He was at the time living in a back-to-back but was lucky when *Pearson's Magazine* described him as 'the coming richest man in the world'. At the time Marson was earning 30 shillings a week. Eastwood visited him in his lodgings and the pair discussed the article in depth. Now Marson began writing to his benefactor signing himself 'Albert, the future Lord Syerston'. Eventually Eastwood recovered his senses and went to the police. At Leeds Assizes in 1902 prosecuting counsel took the then amazing time of four hours to open the case against Marson who received three years' penal servitude.

Iɴ ᴇᴀʀʟʏ January 1909 Violet Gordon Charlesworth was driving a powerful car near Rhyl, North Wales, when she swerved suddenly, shot through the windscreen and disappeared. Her sister and the chauffeur, Watts, who were also in the car, said they feared she had gone over the cliff. Her family applied for £3,000, the amount for which she was insured, but by 9 February that year there were suggestions that she had caught the train back to London along with her sister. An investigator for the insurance company was also not convinced, saying the body would certainly have snagged on the rocks and that even at high tide the water was too shallow to wash it out to sea. Violet had been gambling on the stock market and was thought to owe around £10,000 to her broker.

In fact she was not dead but in Tobermory in the Highlands where she was living under the name Margaret MacLeod and where she was recognised by the village baker who went to the police. Now it all became very complicated: she denied she was Violet, her sister denied it was she, her brother declared she was his sister.

Shortly after her reappearance she rejected a 'blank cheque' from the impresario Oscar Ashe to appear in American musicals. More to her liking was an appearance at Collins Music Hall in Islington at a fee of £300 a week. At the time, temporarily famous people were regularly offered spots on bills. That year Jack Binns, the heroic wireless operator who remained at his post on the sinking of the SS *Republic*, turned down £200.

There again Violet had written a song, 'Good bye Girlie, I must go', albeit one which the *Weekly News* thought bore a striking resemblance to 'Goodbye Dolly Grey'. Her debut was not a success. To mixed cheers and boos she appeared on the stage, said she had a cold, could not sing and retired.

Violet, and her mother Miriam, appeared at Derby Assizes in February 1910 charged with conspiring to defraud Dr Edward Hughes Jones from Rhyl. Jones had been led to believe Violet was due to inherit a substantial sum, somewhere between £75,000 and a quarter of a million and had advanced her loans against it. He also rather thought he was her fiancé. As a come-on she had written 'Ye ken laddie that all my fortune will be yours' on her letter paper which was headed *Mors Portia Macula* –'Death rather than a stain'.

The money was apparently due to come from a man called McDonald whom she had met at a ball in England. The date on which she was to receive this money varied, but one was 13 January 1909. Sometimes Violet thought it might not be until Christmas. She had strung the broker along with the story that if her trustees found out she had been gambling on the market it might delay the inheritance.

Giving evidence, Miriam Charlesworth said she had no reason to doubt her daughter's story as she was a truthful girl.

For a time, it looked as though Mrs Charlesworth might get away with it, claiming it was all Violet's fault and she had been duped as much as anyone else, but Mr Justice Darling would have none of it. He called a doctor from Derby back to the witness box who told the jury Mrs Charlesworth had been running the inheritance story while Violet was still in short frocks. The pair received five years apiece, reduced to three because of the ill health of Mrs Charlesworth.

At the time of her trial a racehorse was named 'Violet Charlesworth' after her; it ran indifferently in National Hunt races for the next ten years. The animal hated having her mane and tail plaited and could only be backed with any confidence when this had not been done.

Charles Wells

THE LASTING CLAIM to fame of Charles Wells, one of the great fraudsmen of his time, is that he was the 'Man who broke the bank at Monte Carlo'.

In fact he did not break the bank, only the pockets of many of his supporters. In July 1891 the 50-year-old Wells had a remarkable run at the tables in Monte Carlo. He had been a small-time conman who received two years for fraud in Paris on 18 December 1885. In the month of his success he turned a stake of £50 into something around £100,000. True, he wiped out a table a dozen times but that was far from breaking the bank. He returned later in the year and proceeded to do the same thing again.

Back in London he raised money to finance another run at the tables. It is a measure of his charm that no one asked him why, since he was a winner from the first turn of the wheel, he needed additional finance. But, off he went again, this time with a yacht and his current girlfriend and lost all his backers' money.

Wells was extradited from France in January 1893. He had been trying to sell his yacht to a Russian in Le Havre for £20,000, something he said he would have been able to do had the arrival of the police not interrupted the transaction.

Described as a patent agent, he was accused of obtaining £28,000 from various investors. Gambling aside, since 1885 he had filed 192 applications for patents but had only completed the formalities in 27 of them. His fraudulent inventions and modifications included torpedoes, hot-air engines, a scheme to save coal on steam vessels and – more modestly – umbrellas, the preservation of mixed mustards and musical skipping ropes. He received eight years.

This lengthy term of imprisonment did nothing at all to cure him. In 1905 under the name of William Davenport and working with a bankrupt clergyman, Vyvyan Henry Moyle, he set up the South and

South West Coast Steam Trading and Fishing Syndicate raising mortgage bonds on a fleet said to be worth £4,000. The fleet consisted of two unseaworthy trawlers which might, just, have fetched £500. Three years for Wells and 18 months for the 71-year-old vicar.

In prison Wells clearly captivated the experienced governor, Sir Basil Thompson:

> [Wells was] the pleasantest and most unselfish of all the men that passed through my hands. He believed that he was not simply a swindler but genuinely believed he would make everyone's fortune. If when I had met him he had been a free man and I had been in possession of money to invest and Wells had held me with his glittering eye and discoursed fluently on his latest project for making money he would have defrauded even me who has a fairly large acquaintance amongst fraudulent company promoters, so great is the power of persuasion of the man who believes in himself.

Wells died aged 85 in 1926. By then he had admitted his roulette winnings were not due to any system but simply to an amazing run of good luck.

Your money and your life

ON 28 FEBRUARY 1917 11-year-old Harry Birkett returned from a day on a Sydney beach to find his mother, Annie, had left their home. His rather uncouth stepfather, Harry Crawford, told him there had been a tiff and that she had gone to stay with friends in North Sydney. Soon after, Crawford sold the furniture and moved out. Harry's stepsister Josephine went to live in the city and he was sent to live with an aunt who began questioning him about his mother and father.

Back in 1911 housekeeper Annie Birkett, then a widow with a son, had been courted by Crawford, a coachman in Wahroonha. It was not an ideal match. He drank and she was looking for better things but none was on offer and in 1915 they began living together in Balmain where she had bought a sweetshop. Later Crawford produced Josephine, his 16-year-old daughter from a previous marriage, and they all went to live together in Drummoyne.

Two weeks after her disappearance, Annie's badly charred body was found in Lane Cove and was identified from a green stone pendant and a dental plate. Crawford disappeared only to be found two years later when he married in Canterbury. He was put on trial for Annie Birkett's murder, and then it all began to unravel.

Harry Crawford was in fact a woman, Eugenie Fellini, born in Florence, Italy, on 23 July 1886. Her parents emigrated to New Zealand and at the age of 16 she signed on as a cabin boy. On board was another Italian and by the end of the trip Eugenie was pregnant. After the birth of Josephine she continued to find work as a man.

Her defence at her trial in Darlinghurst, Sydney, in October 1920 was that there had been no quarrel and, as far as she knew, Annie Birkett was still alive and well. It cut no ice and she was found guilty of murder, sentenced to death, reprieved and released in 1931. After that she ran a boarding house in Paddington under the name of Mrs

Ford. On 10 June 1938 she was knocked down by a car and died from her injuries. So far as the relationship with Annie and the subsequent marriage were concerned, they had been maintained by what were delicately referred to as 'mechanical means'.

On 25 October 1979 Audrey Marie Hilley was indicted for the attempted murder of her daughter Carole and a cheque fraud in Alabama. In November she disappeared from the Birmingham hotel where she was on bail. Meanwhile, she was also indicted for poisoning her husband, Frank.

As Robbi Hannon she turned up in Fort Lauderdale where, in February 1980, she met John Holman and went with him to Marlow, New Hampshire to work as a secretary. They married in May 1981 but it was not a marriage that lasted as she was 'seeking space' and within a month moved to Texas, from where she telephoned Holman both as herself and her non-existent twin sister Terri. Later Robbi went to Florida where, sadly, she died.

She then reappeared as her identical twin sister Terri about whom she had told Holman so much. He introduced her to co-workers at Central Screw where he worked, but some were not convinced and began checking on her background. It turned out that the hospital to which Robbi had apparently left her organs did not exist and neither did the church to which she was said to have belonged in Texas. The police were called in.

Audrey/Robbi/Terri was arrested in January 1983 and received a life sentence for the murder of her first husband and 20 years for the attempted murder of her daughter. She was given home leave on 19 February 1987 and promptly disappeared, but was found suffering from hypothermia on a porch in Anniston, Alabama on 26 February and died that afternoon after a heart attack. Apart from the murder of her husband Frank, she was suspected of the murder of her mother-in-law and a playmate of her daughter. She is also thought to have administered poison to detectives who came to question her.

Until his death following a robbery at a hotel where he then worked, her second husband John always maintained he believed that Terri was indeed a twin sister.

SOMETIMES the French exported their bogus aristocracy, at least once with fatal effects. Henri Perreau, a man of some considerable charm and talent, was a waiter in Paris when in the summer of 1867 he was befriended by a William Cotton who engaged him to show him the sights of the city. When this proved to be a success Cotton took him to Constantinople as a guide. One evening the pair left their hotel and neither returned.

Perreau did eventually reappear, however, this time at the Prince of Wales Hotel, Scarborough – where he was no longer a waiter as he had been in Paris. Rather, he was now Count Henri de Tourville, and in this guise he courted Henrietta Bingham, due to receive an inheritance of £30,000 on the death of her mother. Mrs Bingham must have though it odd that the Count had to borrow from her to finance the honeymoon, but she did not have to worry for long because, on their return, he shot her. The coroner's verdict was one of misadventure. A series of complaining letters was sent to the police and a Scotland Yard detective was sent to investigate. Unfortunately it was the corrupt officer Nathaniel Druscovich, later jailed for his part in a racing swindle, who was promptly bribed by the Count. No further action was taken.

Sadly, Henrietta did not last too long either. They had a son and afterwards she fell ill and died of natural causes, having taken the precaution of leaving the bulk of her fortune to the child. The infant nearly died in a fire that burned down the house and was only saved by the bravery of a police constable who defied the flames. The insurance company declined to pay out.

Afterwards de Tourville came to London where he charmed his way into society. He took a houseboat on the river, could be seen at Ascot and Goodwood and read for the Bar. He also took the trouble to anglicise his first name.

By now he was again running out of funds when he met a widow, Madeleine Miller, who had the not inconsiderable income of £7,000 a year. They married in November 1875 but, again sadly, she did not survive the honeymoon. They went on holiday to the Tyrol with her maid where the happy couple took a coach to the Stelvio Pass. It was such a fine day that they dismissed the coachman and walked back down the pass. Only de Tourville survived the walk. Although there were signs that his wife's body had been dragged over the edge of the Pass, the coroner's verdict was that she had committed suicide. Back in London, de Tourville may have been home but he was not free. The Austrian police had not given up and he was arrested at a London dinner party. Despite the spirited efforts of his counsel Montagu Williams, he was extradited to Austria. It is not recorded whether Williams, in the circumstances, was obliged to observe the courtesy of appearing for a fellow barrister without payment. What is recorded is that de Tourville was sentenced to death but was reprieved and the sentence commuted to one of 'perpetual imprisonment'.

CATHERINE FLANAGAN and Margaret Higgins, two Irish sisters living in Skirving Street, Liverpool, began their insurance racket in 1880. In December that year Catherine's son John died from consumption and the insurance company paid out £71. The next year Margaret Jennings, the daughter of a lodger named Patrick, also died and Mary, Margaret Higgins' eight-year-old stepdaughter, became ill. In November 1882 Mary died.

Flanagan and Higgins then moved to 105 Latimer Street and moved again in September 1883 to Ascot Street. There they arranged that Thomas Higgins, Margaret's husband, should be insured for £100 at a time when a weekly wage was around 15 shillings, but he was drunk when he failed a medical examination to insure him for an extra £50. He died on 2 October that year and when his brother Patrick went to collect the insurance money he found it had already been drawn. He went to the coroner and the funeral was stopped. On exhumation and examination, arsenic was found in all the bodies. The women were arrested and duly hanged together on 5 March 1884.

What is more surprising is that this was the tip of an iceberg. In north-west England there was a whole industry at the time, and Flanagan and Higgins were not the first. In 1878 Ellen Heesom killed her mother and two of her children after insuring them. Catherine Flanagan had actually brought a successful libel action, when she was awarded £5, against a local undertaker who alleged she had poisoned her husband and two sons. After her conviction, Flanagan told the authorities of two other poisoners and three further women involved in the insurance end of the business, giving details of six further victims. However, there were no more prosecutions, principally because Higgins and Flanagan were close to five out of the six people, and the police thought there was every likelihood of the other women being acquitted.

Two GRIFTING grannies are currently awaiting trial in California in a very similar case which shows nothing has really changed. Originally held on fraud charges, the two women, aged 73 and 75, have now been charged with murder for financial gain of two homeless men, for which they may face the death penalty. Police believe they hatched a scheme to offer them shelter, and then to collect more than $2 million from the insurance policies after they were killed in hit-and-run crashes. In November 1999 and June 2005 both victims were knocked down in alleys in the early hours and no witnesses have been found. The women allegedly paid the men's rent for nearly two years in exchange for obtaining the victims' signatures and opening at least a dozen life insurance policies with themselves named as beneficiaries. Police believe they may also have arranged the accidents and that they were befriending other men for the future to do the same to them.

In March 2007 the pair pleaded not guilty and the indictments were dismissed on a technicality. The women's triumph was short-lived. The prosecution brought new indictments and were said to be still considering whether to seek the death penalty. The proceedings continue.

On 16 January 2002 Curtis Wharton and his wife Sheila from Shreeveport, Louisiana were attacked on a lonely road near Port-au-Prince, Haiti, when hijackers stopped their car. When she refused to get out they shot her, threw her out and drove off, leaving a distraught Wharton by the roadside. On investigation the police were surprised to find that although her jewellery was gone the thieves had not taken a camera, a computer or credit cards.

It all came about from watching too much television. In December 1997 Curtis Wharton, who had an insurance business, saw a programme about an insurance fraud involving the faked death of a wife. When he met and married Sheila later that month he persuaded her to go along with the idea of a similar insurance fraud.

Over a period of months they took out life insurance policies totalling $2 million on Sheila. Mostly, Curtis was the beneficiary but some money was to go to his secretary, Judy Nipper. Although Curtis had now obtained a false passport for her, Sheila developed cold feet and wanted to back out. Curtis Wharton, made of sterner stuff, then hired a hitman in Haiti, paid him $7,500 and had her killed while they were on a business holiday there. He received two life sentences and Judy Nipper, who had been transferring the necessary cash to Wharton in Haiti, a little under five years.

MICHAEL MALLOY, whose only claim to fame was the manner of his death, was murdered on 22 February 1933 in an insurance swindle. A Bronx saloon owner, Tony Marino, together with his chief barman Archie Mott and two customers Daniel Kriegsberg and Frank Pasqua, chose Malloy, a vagrant, to be the victim of their second swindle. The first had been Betty Carlson the previous year.

In Carlson's case they had plied this relatively attractive young woman with drink and arranged for her to have a room in a nearby lodging house. Willing to please her benefactors she signed papers which she understood were to propose Marino as mayor. In fact she was signing an insurance policy application for $2,000 in his favour. Rendered completely drunk she was left in her room naked, with cold water poured on her and the window open. She died on 17 March 1932 from what the coroner certified as pneumonia brought on by alcoholism.

The 55-year-old Malloy was a much tougher man altogether. He too was picked off the streets and over a period of time plied with drink. His life was insured for $3,500 under a double-indemnity clause as Marino's aim was to recoup only $1,750 and so avoid suspicion.

Malloy steadily resisted their efforts to get him to drink himself to death, flourishing on the free and limitless alcohol. Next he was given what was probably antifreeze mixed in with the liquor. He collapsed but, in apparent good health, re-emerged from his room at the back of the bar within an hour. He was then fed an increasingly strong quantity of antifreeze together with horse liniment mixed with rat poison, but it appeared to have no effect on the man's iron constitution. According to the stories he was next fed with oysters poisoned with raw alcohol, again to no effect. Various other efforts were made to dispose of him including leaving him naked, but this time in Crotona Park. He survived after being found by the police and given a new set of clothes.

He was also thrown from a cab and when that failed an effort was made to find a professional hitman. Unfortunately he appears to have wanted $500, now well beyond the means of the conspirators. Finally, Malloy was successfully gassed on 23 February 1933 and Marino and the others managed to obtain a certificate saying he had died from pneumonia. By this time, however, they had involved too many people, including the cab driver and the thwarted hitman, who began to complain about not being paid for their work. Marino and the others were executed during June and July 1934 at Sing Sing prison.

Alvin Clarence 'Titanic' Thompson

A VERSION OF HOW Alvin Clarence Thompson, one of the twentieth century's great exponents of the short con, became known as 'Titanic' was that he escaped from the sinking vessel dressed in women's clothes, and that he and colleagues then began a series of fraudulent claims against the vessel's insurance company. It is more likely, however, that shortly after the *Titanic* sank Thompson appeared in Joplin, Missouri, where he not only cleaned up at poker but also won $500 by betting he could jump across a pool table without touching it – he dived head first. A local gambler, asking his name was told, 'It must be Titanic. He sinks everybody.'

Born in 1892 Thompson is reputed to have begun his career as a small boy, betting a stranger his dog could retrieve any stone from a pond. The man marked one with an 'X', threw it in the pond and the dog duly brought it back. Thompson claimed he had marked all the stones in the pond the night before. As an adult he won money betting he could drive a golf ball 500 yards, which he did – across a frozen lake. On another occasion he bet local gamblers that the sign which said 'Joplin – 20 Miles' was wrong and that Joplin was only 15 miles away. He had dug up and replaced the signpost five miles closer to the town. He was an excellent golfer who could have turned professional but he preferred the adrenalin rush of gambling. He would play golf right handed, lose narrowly and then bet heavily on himself in a return the next day agreeing to play left handed, which he was. He also beat the world champion horseshoe thrower. The man believed he was playing on a regulation-sized court but Thompson had extended it by a foot.

In 1928 he was a big winner in the crooked poker game in which the gambler Arnold Rothstein, who had fixed baseball's 1919 World Series, dropped $475,000 and was found shot dead six weeks later. Thompson gave evidence when George McManus, who had organised the game and was charged with Rothstein's murder, was acquitted. For a conman anonymity is the name of the game and, with his name and face now famous after the trial, the easy money dried up. Thompson spent the next 30 years moving around the country playing cards and golf, but the great days were gone. The six-times-married Thompson died almost penniless near Fort Worth, Texas, in 1974. He is said to be the model for the gambler Sky Masterson in *Guys and Dolls*.

All the fun of the fair

JUST AS IT IS SAID that Elvis Presley, Princess Diana, JFK, Lord Lucan, Butch Cassidy and several dozen others are alive and living together on a remote island in the mid-Atlantic, there have been continuing stories that the actor John Wilkes Booth, the assassin of President Lincoln, survived his shooting at Garratts Farm, Virginia, on 26 April 1865 – 12 days after Lincoln's death. One story is that he went to act in San Francisco, another that he became a Texas saloon keeper and, most improbably, that he went to Bombay where he was still alive in 1879.

In 1903 David George from Enid, Oklahoma, announced shortly before his death that he was Booth. The claim was dubious, first because he was much taller than Booth and second, his eyes were blue, as opposed to the actor's, which everyone agreed were black. Nevertheless the story gained some credence and a Memphis lawyer, Finis L. Bates, bought the corpse, had it mummified and sent it out for exhibition at fairs and in circuses. Over the years the body had an adventurous life. It was repeatedly bought and sold, seized for debt, kidnapped for ransom and, in the 1930s, X-rayed – with inconclusive results – in an effort to prove it really was Booth. It disappeared, or disintegrated, sometime after 1972.

At least the body did not suffer the indignities heaped on that of the genuine, if unsuccessful, outlaw Elmer McCurdy, shot in 1911. His corpse ended up painted in Day-Glo hanging by his neck in the 'Laff in the Dark' ghost train tunnel in a Long Beach fairground in 1976.

THE STAR TURN on the fairground at the Royal Sydney Show in 1935 was 'The World's Strangest Phantasm', a headless woman, no less than a princess born in Gallegoe, South Patagonia. She appeared before the spectators in a glass dome on a couch in a black dress and surrounded by black curtains, fed by a Frankenstein-like array of drips and tubes around her neck. Indeed so strange was she that her next engagement was to be before 'medical scientists in London who would be gathering to examine her'. Members of the audience in Sydney were given rather less than two minutes each to look at, but certainly not to examine, the Princess. In fact, such was her success that her next appearance was not in London but at a series of country fairs in New South Wales, which came to an abrupt end when the exhibit was raided by the police in Coonamble. The 'Princess' was a long-necked runaway boy aged 17 whose head was hidden by a curtain. He was taken to the Children's Court and later found a proper job. The police issued a short statement: 'As far as the public is concerned the Princess is dead.'

CARNIVAL swindles need not be expensive to execute. It is often only necessary to adapt to the circumstances: if you have been tattooed make the most of it. At the traditional Barnet Horse Fair in September 1922 the police arrested a mother and daughter for fraud. Their booth carried the placard: 'First German atrocity shown in England. See what a mother will suffer for her children. Only ladies allowed to touch the body.'

The story was that during the First World War, when this Belgian mother would not tell the Germans where she had hidden her daughters, she had been 'arrested' as a spy. For the sport of some of the officers, a young French artist had been forced to tattoo her from head to foot. PC Mizen found the older woman in a mask with the upper part of her body swathed in a sheet and the lower part tattooed with designs. 'When I questioned her she admitted she was a London woman who had never been to Belgium.' The woman was fined £1 and her daughter was bound over to be of good behaviour.

IN THE 1930s, the Great Mortado, the Human Fountain, 'The only living man captured by savages and actually crucified', appeared regularly in fairs all over the US. During his act he allowed nails to be driven through the holes in his hands and feet, producing realistic bleeding by bursting sacks of red ink. Using a specially plumbed chair he shot jets of water through them. Mortado had actually had the holes bored in his hands and feet and to keep them from healing over he was obliged to have wooden plugs inserted. Years later a man was found crucified in a New York subway. It was thought that perhaps it was Mortado's final appearance.

Thirty years earlier in the 1890s, Tommy Minnock, known in the trade as a 'horse', or one impervious to pain, sang with his head on one side, 'After the Ball was Over' while in 'similitude of the picture of the crucifixion of Christ' in music halls in New Jersey. Unsurprisingly, he was an outstanding success. Minnock had been a pupil of Jean-Martin Charcot, the French hypnotist, and could fake catalepsy by greatly reducing his heart beat. He would also allow his eyeball to be thumped and his body to be pierced. Additionally he could eat vast quantities of cayenne pepper. When Charcot died in 1893 he left Minnock enough money to return to the US where he worked with a variety of mentalists, faith healers and hypnotists, including J.H. Loryea, who, as Santanelli, staged the crucifixion act.

Descents from the Cross had been part of illusionists' acts since the American Civil War, but the stunt was not without its dangers. In September 1943 the German, or Swiss-born, Harry Von Weickede died shortly after being crucified, despite being hospitalised. In 1955 the Venezuelan Ernesto Vilcher, billed as 'Chami Khan' and described as a 'spiritual descendant of the Indian Fakir Tradition', was introduced by the Rev. Don Bodley of Detroit before he was crucified in Sturgis, Michigan, breaking the world record of 100 hours. He was still undertaking the act in 1962 when he was billed to appear in Los Angeles.

Even more interesting was the Trinidadian Evatina Tardo, who, in the 1920s, had amazing ability to withstand pain, allowing poisonous snakes to bite her bare arms. Sometimes the venom would be extracted and injected into a rabbit which would immediately die in agony. Said to be exceptionally beautiful, she claimed she was able to stop her heartbeat for up to six minutes. Her story was that she had been bitten as a child on the island and so had immunity; the difficulty that snakes are not indigenous to Trinidad was overlooked. Harry Houdini thought her immunity was due to having an absolutely empty stomach before her act and immediately drinking milk after being bitten. She was another who would be nailed to a cross where she would hang for over two hours singing and talking to the audience. Ms Tardo had the nails dipped in poison and she claimed, 'There wouldn't be any fun unless I had prussic acid on the ends.'

One of the great 1933 Christmas attractions at Jones Brothers store in the Holloway Road, North London, was the Princess Ubangi, 30 inches high and Queen of the Pygmies. Her manager, Joe Gardiner, had her appearing in the store for four weeks, during which time 13,800 people paid threepence each to see her dance and, as a police report put it, 'act up'. She had moved to Kennards in Croydon by the time the authorities received a letter from South Africa to say that neither Gardiner nor the Princess were all they might be and he had already promoted her as the Japanese Princess Kameda in South Africa. More recently he had been trying to find investors to finance the sending of a pig to England which, he claimed, the Prince of Wales would ride at Wembley.

When the police interviewed the Princess during a break she admitted she was not the Queen of the Pygmies and that she could not climb a tree; she was 26-year-old Maria Peters, a Cape Coloured. She had signed a five-year contract with Gardiner who paid her lodgings and £8 a month; now she was exhausted and wanted to go home. A doctor was called and an examination showed she had a growth on her pelvis and should not go on dancing. The crowd had thrown £1. 2s 3d into her enclosure and she insisted that the doctor's fee of 10s 6d be paid from it. When Gardiner was told the police were closing the show he threatened them with his solicitors. In turn they considered a prosecution, but nothing came of either. The police officers received a commendation for 'Skill and ability in a case of improper exploitation of a human female monstrosity.'

ONE OF SHOWMAN P.T. Barnum's greatest hoaxes was the Feejee Mermaid, obtained in 1842 'from the Feejee Islands and preserved in China'. Punters were more than happy to pay 25 cents admission to see a dried and withered specimen that had some human and some fishy characteristics. It was, Barnum later admitted, the upper part of a monkey and the tail of a fish.

Perhaps the most famous of all Barnum's exhibits was the midget 'General' Tom Thumb, born in London. In fact, he was Charles Sherwood Stratton, born in Connecticut on 4 January 1838 and was aged four when he was first recruited. His father was a carpenter and his mother worked at a local inn. The child was, unsurprisingly, extremely shy and took all of a week to train. By the time he was nine he had toured Europe and been presented to Queen Victoria on three occasions. His bride, another midget – Lavinia Warren Bump (the last name was soon dropped) – was born in 1841 and was 21 when she met Stratton. The couple were exhibited for weeks before the wedding, which took place on 10 February 1863 at the Grace Church, New York. Naturally there had to be offspring and on 5 December that year it was announced that Lavinia had given birth. The child was in fact borrowed from a foundling home and, over the years and tours, English babies were used in England, French babies in France and so on. Tom Thumb died on 15 July 1883. Lavinia married again, this time another small person, Count Primo Magri, and founded the Lilliputian Opera Company, eventually playing at Midget City on Coney Island. She died aged 78 in 1919.

After the First World War, Horace Ridler, a prep-school-educated army officer who served with the Desert Mountain Corps in Mesopotamia and was decorated for bravery, squandered his fortune, took up farming and went broke again. In 1922 he went to the celebrated tattooist 'Professor' George Burchett and had himself tattooed with zebra stripes, something which, at two inches a day, took a year. He maintained he paid Burchett £5,000 but the tattooist said he had charged only £1,500 and was never paid in full. In 1927, claiming to have been forcibly tattooed by natives in New Guinea, Rider began a successful career in the circus as 'The Great Omi: the Zebra Man' with his wife Gladys as Omette. Ten years later he appeared on Broadway and then toured with the Ringling Brothers. He applied to re-enlist during the Second World War but was rejected and spent the duration exhibiting himself for war charities. He died in Sussex in 1969 aged 81.

SHORTLY BEFORE the First World War, the carnival barker and, later, Hollywood publicist Harry Reichenbach exhibited a bowl of water containing 'The Only Living Brazilian Invisible Fish' in the window of a restaurant which was apparently doing badly. Crowds would watch the water, which from time to time would be blown by a hidden fan, and shout, 'Look there it is.' The story goes that the punters would then go into the restaurant which became hugely successful. Other versions of the story are that he had the exhibit at a fairground.

When he was invited to act as publicity agent for the silent-screen actor Francis X. Bushman in order to build him up prior to contract negotiations, Reichenbach arranged to meet him at the station and walk to the film studios with him. By the time they arrived they were followed by an excited crowd and Bushman was able to use this as a demonstration of his popularity. More to the point, Reichenbach had been dropping a continuous stream of coins behind them during the mile-long walk.

Among his other tricks, when he was promoting a vaudeville show he paid a beggar to accost one of the chorus girls. When the man was brought up in court later that night she 'discovered' he was her long-lost father – for that evening at least. The next night a woman ran down the aisle of the theatre to tell another girl, 'Marge, your baby is dying.' The girl leaped over the footlights in her underwear and for the rest of the evening sat sobbing at the hospital while photographers took pictures – until the infant was returned to its rightful owners.

Reichenbach is one of the hustlers to whom the 'Dancing Ducks' are attributed. The birds apparently danced more or less in time to 'Turkey in the Straw'. In fact, the poor things were trying to remove their feet from heated plates.

THE FIRST 'Wild Men from Borneo' appeared in the 1850s. Generally they were black youths from the southern states trained to wear tusks. One had a silver plate inserted under his skin and when he was on display horns were screwed on. The best known in California in the late nineteenth century was, however, a white man in a freak show on San Francisco's waterfront. 'Captured and imported at enormous expense,' he was covered in road tar and horsehair, kept in a cage and fed raw meat. From time to time he would rattle the bars and yell what seemed to be 'Oofty Goofty'. Unfortunately he could not perspire through the tar and hair and had to be taken to hospital where tar solvent was poured on him, and he was put on the hospital roof to melt.

After that he took to singing, with little talent, in beer halls and variety houses and appeared as Romeo, with an obese prostitute Big Bertha as Juliet, at the Bella Union Hall. Another known in the trade as a 'horse', he would allow himself to be beaten at 50 cents a hit. One who took up the offer was the pugilist John L. Sullivan who, in

1890, gave him a bad beating. He died six years later and it had to be made clear that Sullivan was not responsible for his death. The Wild Man's true identity was never disclosed.

Changes of identity were often needed for wild men. When the hirsute Glasgow-born Milton Reed, who wrestled as 'Jungle Boy', suffered from *alopaecia totalis* he quickly became the hairless 'Mighty Chang'. In 1997 one of a long line of professional wrestlers who appeared as the 'Wild Man of Borneo', Bill Olivas, was ordained as a Catholic priest in California at the age of 76.

WHEN P.T. Barnum wished to clear the crowds from his emporium to make room for the next wave he had a sign erected To THE EGRESS. Those who pushed through the door in the hope of seeing a gigantic black woman merely found themselves in the street.

Big Bertha Heyman and Cassie Chadwick

CONFIDENCE TRICKS and tricksters of both sexes come in all shapes, sizes and ages. Take Bertha Heyman, known as 'Big Bertha', who was regarded by Inspector Thomas Byrnes as one of the smartest confidence women in the US. This was despite the fact that she was a somewhat unprepossessing-looking woman weighing 245 pounds and standing only 5 feet 4 inches tall, with four prominent moles on her right cheek. Her father had served five years in Posen, Poland, for forgery by the time she arrived in the US, at the age of 27, in 1878. She married a Fritz Karko and then, bigamously, a Mr Heyman in Milwaukee who seems to have been dropped from the picture pretty swiftly.

In 1880 she was sued in the New York civil courts over a claim for $1,035. Two criminal trials followed the next year when she was acquitted in London, Ontario and Staten Island. As she left the second court she was rearrested and charged with a string of offences of obtaining money by false pretences, for which she received two years. She was employed as a servant in the warden's quarters and there made the acquaintance of a German, Charles Karpe, who took to visiting her. While still in prison she relieved him of his life savings of $900. On her release in 1883 she swindled a firm of New York brokers, pretending that a sealed package of worthless papers was worth $87,000. She had the nerve to say she was worth $8 million and was believed, at least until the packet was opened. She was arrested in July that year and received five years on 22 August. Byrnes consid ered she possessed 'a wonderful knowledge of human nature and can deceive those who consider themselves particularly shrewd in business'.

Age does not discriminate against conwomen, one of the most talented of whom, Cassie Chadwick, flourished into her middle age. She came upon the scene in the 1890s and moved into Cleveland society with the story that she was the illegitimate daughter of the philanthropist Andrew Carnegie. She had with her a number of promissory notes apparently signed by the steel magnate. Her initial trick, which was only a variation of one worked by so many, was to go to Carnegie's house and pretend to be received. The only person she actually saw was the housekeeper. The dupe, this time a lawyer, waited in the carriage outside but he was then in a position to give credibility to her story that she had access to Carnegie.

Swearing her banker to secrecy, which was, of course, the best way of ensuring her tale was told, she took out some loans of around $100,000 which she repaid by borrowing from other banks. For a period of some seven years she entertained and was entertained, travelled to Europe and became a major benefactress. Then, in 1904, one of her creditors did what perhaps should have been done a decade earlier – he had her background checked. Since she was actually the Canadian forger Elizabeth Bigley, it was not surprising that the promissory notes signed by Carnegie had looked so good. On 26 November her story appeared in the Cleveland press and the game was up.

She was arrested in bed in the New Breslin Hotel, New York, and after a spell in the Tombs was taken back to Cleveland. She received ten years and died in prison on 10 October 1907. Charles T. Beckwith, president of the Citizens National Bank of Oberlin, predeceased her. His bank was owed $1.25 million dollars by her and, on hearing the news, he promptly had a heart attack. In all it is thought she took in excess of $20 million from a number of banks.

Very well insured

TWENTY-THREE-YEAR-OLD club bouncer Andreas Plack's great 2001 money-making scheme went sadly awry when his cousin, Cristian Kleos, agreed to mutilate Plack's leg with a chainsaw in woods near Bolsano, Italy. The goal was insurance of £330,000 and a disability pension. After Kleos had done the hard cutting he went off to drop the chainsaw in the river Adige. Plack was to call the emergency services on his mobile telephone, but unfortunately Kleos had severed one of his cousin's major arteries and all the operator heard was a faint mumble followed by a death rattle. The people of Bolsano feared there was a maniac on the loose until Kleos was arrested and confessed.

PLAYING WITH fire can also be a bad idea. In the US two brothers were hired in 2004 to set a car on fire so that the owner could collect on the insurance. They doused it with petrol and, to make doubly sure the car would be destroyed, they threw in a pipe bomb. The bomb instantly exploded, setting one of the men on fire and killing him. His brother had rushed to help him, but ended up catching on fire himself. When the police arrived he confessed what they had been up to before he, too, passed away.

TONY BAILEY, who claimed he suffered back injuries when he slipped while working at a mushroom farm in Dorset in April 2002, could have netted £1 million in compensation from the company's insurers. He claimed he was incontinent and unable to walk, lying to doctors about his injuries and making his partner push him around in a wheelchair. He even went on a caravan holiday by the sea, telling his solicitors he was going into respite care. However, after private investigators filmed him walking around Yeovil town centre and driving to a supermarket – echoing *Little Britain*'s supposedly wheelchair-bound character Andy – he admitted conspiracy to defraud and was given a prison sentence of three and a half years.

STAFF IN A supermarket were so concerned when a Somerset man slipped and fell on spilt shampoo in October 2001 that they insisted he should go straight to hospital, even putting the three teeth he had knocked out into a glass of milk in the hope they could be re-implanted. It was only when the store received a solicitor's letter for compensation that they reviewed their closed-circuit television tape, which showed the man squirting the shampoo on the floor. Horrified by the bill from the dentist who had extracted the rotten teeth earlier, he had driven to the supermarket clutching them in a bloodstained tissue and faked the fall, hoping the store would pick up the tab. He received a year's community service from South Somerset magistrates.

AT THE BEGINNING of the twentieth century, American Edward Pape had a genuinely broken neck but instead of working in sideshows and circuses he earned his considerable living falling off trolleys and tramcars and suing the unfortunate owners. He had the ability to fall and roll into the gutter as the car was slowing to a stop. Examination would show he had broken his neck and a quick cash settlement rather than a lengthy and expensive law suit followed.

SOME CONMEN have earned their money painfully. In the late 1890s Campbell and Henderson travelled the whole of Australia swindling railway companies. Their modus operandi was to fall out of trains deliberately and then blame the railway company for leaving the door open. They began with a couple of failures in Victoria and Tasmania but they learned their lessons well. They next visited South Australia where they picked up £350 and then moved on to Western Australia where the takings amounted to £750. Greed was their un doing when they claimed £10,000 in Queensland. It was really too large an amount even if, as he claimed, Campbell had been paralysed from the feet upwards. He must have had an extraordinary tolerance of pain for, in a test to determine whether he had been injured, 'extreme electrical appliances were used but he never flinched'. His conduct was regarded as a marvel of endurance by the experts. He failed the test when it was applied above the seat of the injury and he did not even flinch then. Each received seven years' imprisonment.

A SPECIALIST IN trips and tumbles, for 15 years beginning in her late fifties, Isabel Parker made a good living out of falling in supermarkets throughout New Jersey and Pennsylvania. Customers would find this late-middle-aged lady, who chose stores without security cameras, lying or sitting in an aisle rubbing her back or neck. Claims followed and were usually settled following calls from her cell phone. When insurance investigators wished to interview Granny Parker the claim was dropped.

The incident which put at least a temporary halt to her career came when she was found by the owner of a Philadelphia liquor store after she had apparently fallen over a three-feet-high pile of cardboard. Neither the store owner nor the insurance investigator were convinced by her story, and it turned out that Granny Parker was already serving four years' house arrest over a series of 29 thefts and insurance frauds in New Jersey. To carry out her scams she had used eight telephone numbers, 11 different addresses, 47 aliases and 32 Social Security numbers. This time she received probation.

SOMETIMES victims of confidence tricksters are buried, but it is rare that an eight-ton mechanical cotton picker suffers the same fate. In 1999 Georgia farmer, Curtis Donald Keene, temporarily unable to pay the HP instalments on his green John Deere truck the size of a dustcart, buried it, reported it stolen and was paid out $102,000. Eight months later a neighbour noticed the John Deere was resurfacing and while insurance workers toiled to excavate it, the neighbourhood watched, sitting on deckchairs and sipping lemonade. The matter was settled when Keene repaid the insurance money.

AN EXTENDED family, the 'Jim Millers', operated an insurance fraud ring in the south-west US in the 1990s. The family made over 145 claims on 12 insurance companies varying from vandals spray-painting their homes, fires, slips and falls in commercial buildings, the slashing of furniture and clothing and being run off the road. In 1995 Miller and 17 relatives and associates were indicted on 23 counts of fraud.

Around the same time in Dublin a man claimed he had fallen over an uneven pavement. An investigation showed that three of his four siblings as well as six cousins had all come to grief at the same spot.

A MAN IN North Carolina insured a box of very rare, expensive cigars against fire. Within a month, having smoked the lot, he contacted the insurance company, claiming he had lost the cigars in 'a series of small fires', which indeed he had. The company refused to pay, citing the obvious reason that the cigars had been consumed in the normal fashion, but the man sued and won. In delivering his ruling, the judge stated that since the man held a policy which had warranted the cigars were insurable against fire without defining what the insurers considered to be 'unacceptable fire', they were obligated to compensate the insured for his loss. Rather than endure a lengthy and costly appeal process the insurance company paid up $15,000, but after the man had cashed his cheque the company had him arrested on 24 counts of arson, using his claim and testimony from the previous case as evidence against him. The man was subsequently convicted of intentionally burning the rare cigars and was sentenced to a year in jail.

This may sound an amazing story – and it is. Although it has been widely circulating since at least 1968 no one has yet managed to establish the source of this urban legend.

Abram Sykowski

I N SEPTEMBER 1946 Count Navarro was arrested when he arrived at Miami airport from Curaçao. The police were delighted. He was, they said, known as 'Kid Tiger' or 'The Frogman' and had been wanted for some years. The Count, had, they added, been running a version of the Spanish Prisoner Swindle since the 1930s, claiming that he had access to safe deposits belonging to Al Capone. Bail was set at the equivalent of £25,000, which he said he could meet, although after some plea bargaining he received only a short sentence.

In fact the Count was the Polish conman Abram Sykowski, born on 23 July 1892. Like his contemporary 'Dapper' Dan Collins, Sykowski, who had the ability to dislocate his limbs, had worked in a circus appearing as 'The Human Frog'. He served short sentences in Havana in 1912 and then served two more for petty forgery. He had not yet found his métier and for a time worked, not with Capone himself, but with his ally, the bootlegger, Ralph Sheldon. He was arrested for theft and served six years before being deported to Germany where he bought and sold arms and arranged passports which never materialised.

It was in 1930 that he originated his Capone bank account scam, explaining it to a casino owner to whom he owed money. In Rome in 1936 he embroidered the benefits to Carla Petacci and her lover, Benito Mussolini, who gave him 7 million lire for a share. In Spain, using the name Carlos Ladenis, he took the police chief of Barcelona for $35,000. Now a Hapsburg prince in Montreal, he took $125,000 from a group of businessmen hoping for their share of the $350 million he had deposited in the US banks.

After he served his sentence in the US he was deported to Cuba in 1949. He then travelled to Paris and the French Riviera where he was the pure, if not simple Antonio Novarro; it was here in April 1952 the playboy King Farouk gave him $200,000 for his share in the Capone account – the king was overthrown before he wasted more money.

A degenerate gambler, Sykowski left the Riviera the next year but he was stopped at the Swiss border and placed under house arrest in Paris. He escaped into West Germany and has never actually been identified again although it appears he continued his high-class frauds unhindered for the next 30 years.

Culture vultures

IN 1983 *The Hitler Diaries* were launched on an unsuspecting public. It was the literary event of the year. The diaries contained intimate recollections by the Führer, such as one at the time of the 1936 Berlin Olympics: 'Hope my stomach cramps don't return during the Games.' The 60 volumes, plus two on Rudolph Hess's flight to Brit-ain, were apparently discovered by Gerd Heidemann, a staff writer on the German magazine *Stern*, who was able to buy them from a Dr Fischer. In turn, they had come from an East German farmer who had found them in a crashed Nazi aeroplane.

Apart from the intimacy of the Führer's gastric problems, the diaries showed him in a better light than was generally thought. He was unaware of the concentration camps and wanted to resettle the Jewish population, not exterminate them.

Bells should have rung. Dr Fischer was none other than the German painter and military antiques dealer, Konrad Kujau, who as a child had forged the autographs of politicians and had later produced a sequel to *Mein Kampf*. Of all the so-called paintings by Hitler he is thought to have produced at least a quarter.

It was, however, a question of the victims wanting to believe the diaries were authentic and *Stern* paid around $2.3 million for them. They were sold on to *Newsweek, The Times* and *Sunday Times* after Professor Hugh Trevor-Roper, then a director of Times Newspapers, pronounced them genuine. *Stern* thought that history would have to be rewritten but, before that became necessary, tests on the paper and ink showed that they were fakes.

Kujau was jailed for 42 months, and after his release became a media celebrity, appearing on German television forging Old Masters, but now sensibly adding his own signature. He claimed that most of the money was siphoned off by Heidemann who in turn claimed he had been duped by Kujau, who later stood unsuccessfully for Mayor of Stuttgart. He died of cancer in 2000.

Kujau would have been proud of his great-niece Petra Kujau. In April 2006 she was arrested and charged with selling 500 fake Kujaus, including Canalettos and Monets, to clients worldwide. The prosecution alleged that paintings, bought for as little as ten euros each from art schools in Asia, had the Kujau signature forged, so adding thousands of euros to their value. After the raid by the police the Konrad Kujau Museum in Pfullendorf near Dresden was closed.

NETLEY LUCAS began badly, was seemingly reformed and then went to being bad again. The good-looking youth was expelled for theft and forging his housemaster's signature. There followed a series of court appearances including obtaining credit by fraud. He absconded from a boys' training ship in August 1919, and in July 1920 was arrested in London at the Imperial Hotel, Russell Square where he was masquerading as the Hon. Captain Netley Lucas. He was charged with obtaining credit by fraud from Harrods. He then set up an agency offering young women bogus jobs, a scheme he repeated when he went to Canada after his next release in 1923. He claimed there was 'a trace of insanity in my brain' but the prison doctors would have none of it.

It was then he seemingly reformed: in 1925 writing The *Autobiography of a Crook*, dedicated to 'those who buy this book, thereby giving the author a chance to start afresh'. After that he produced a string of titles including *Crook Janes*, in which he claimed to have met the notorious 'Chicago May' Sharpe. In 1928 he announced his engagement to this 53-year-old woman who was, at the time, living destitute in Philadelphia.

The following year, as Evelyn Graham, he wrote the 'authentic biography' of Lord Justice Darling under His Lordship's 'personal supervision'. And for the next ten years under a string of names such as Lady Angela Stanley and Charlotte Cavendish, and with a string of ghost writers, he produced bestselling biographies of the Prince of Wales, Princess Mary, the King of Spain and Albert, King of the Belgians.

As Lady Angela Stanley, supposedly a former lady-in-waiting to Queen Alexandra, who wanted to write her memoirs, he forged a letter from Lord Stanfordham, then private secretary to George V, saying the royal family thoroughly approved of an autobiography.

Exposed by a national newspaper, he appeared at the Old Bailey where he received 18 months for obtaining £225 – Lady Angela's advance for the book – by false pretences. On his release he wrote, under his own name, another autobiography *Our Selves*. In June 1940 he was found dead in the burned-out lounge of a furnished house he had rented near Leatherhead under the name of Robert Tracey. And with him died Lady Angela, Evelyn Graham, Charlotte Cavendish and a couple of others.

ONE OF THE best-selling novels of the 1960s was *Naked Came the Stranger*, a raunchy tale of a deceived housewife who plans her revenge on her unfaithful husband by having sex with as many neighbourhood men as she can manage. Written by the Long Island housewife Penelope Ashe very much in the style of Jacqueline Susann, it was an enormous success, selling 20,000 copies pre-publication. When Penelope gave interviews she was self-deprecatory about her talents. Well she might have been – the book was actually written by 24 journalists from *Newsweek* who, under the supervision of columnist Mike McGrady, each produced a chapter. McGrady had rejected those that were too-well written. The retiring Penelope Ashe was his sister-in-law. The journalists confessed during an appearance on *The David Frost Show* when they emerged in line with the band playing 'A Pretty Girl is like a Melody'.

By the time the cross-dressing, HIV-infected J.T. Leroy, a child truck-stop prostitute in California, had been cured of a drug habit, she had written, on the advice of her psychiatrist, three books about her life on these mean streets, thinly disguised as fiction. The work of this semi-recluse – whose 2002 novel, *Harold's End*, was the story of the relationship between a heroin-addicted street kid and his pet snail – was highly praised by such diverse talents as Dave Eggars, Zadie Smith and Lou Reed. There were only rare public appearances by the author who declined to read from her work, which was so successful that it was translated into 20 languages. She was another who was rightly reclusive, because J.T. Leroy was the invention of Laura Albert and Geoffrey Knoop, two middle-aged musicians. Appearances were made by Knoop's sister, Savannah, impersonating J.T. Leroy.

Ern Malley, in theory born in 1918 and who died in Australia in 1943, had a short-lived but highly influential career. The total output of his work – 16 poems in a pastiche of Dylan Thomas entitled *The Darkening Ecliptic* – took James McAuley and Harold Stewart a whole afternoon to write. The poems were sent to Max Harris, the 22-year-old editor of the avant-garde magazine *Angry Penguins*, with a covering letter from Ethel, Malley's sister. The letter explained that she had found the poems after her brother's death and while she did not understand them she thought they should be published.

The poems of this genius, who had tragically died so young after a long illness, duly appeared, but the hoax was soon exposed. Not only was the unfortunate Harris deceived, but in September 1945 he was also prosecuted for publishing indecent material. Detective Voelsang, acting for the South Australian police, objected to the poem *Egyptian Register* because it contained the word 'genitals'. He also objected to the word 'incestuous', saying, 'I don't know what that means but I think there is a suggestion of indecency about it.' Harris was fined £5.

Ironically, the poetry, written by McAuley and Stewart to expose the poets they so despised, somehow escaped the control of its creators. Not only has Ern Malley's work had considerable influence on younger Australian poets, but in 1992 the editors of the new *Penguin Book of Modern Australian Poetry* elected to include all the poems in their anthology.

IN 1960 WALTER Lehmann, husband, father and apple farmer in Tasmania, also had a brief literary career, writing only 14 poems through his creator Gwen Harwood, who was tired of not being taken seriously as a poet and believed that there were a great many people who couldn't 'tell a poem from a bunyip's arse'. The *oeuvre* was sent to the magazine *Bulletin,* which duly published them. Two of the poems were acrostics – the first letter of each line read downwards make a phrase or sentence. A sonnet from Eloise to Abelard read, 'SO LONG BULLETIN' while his reply read, 'FUCK ALL EDITORS'. Gwen Harwood was bitterly disappointed when she was described in *Tasmanian Truth* as 'Tas Housewife in Hoax of the Year'.

MARCH 1997 WAS not a good month for the Australian intelligentsia. First, the 47-year-old white male taxi driver Leon Carmen admitted he was actually the author of the acclaimed novel *My Own Sweet Time* by the indigenous Australian prize-winner Wanda Koolmatrie, allegedly of the lost Pitjantjatara people of South Australia. Days later the elderly white painter Elizabeth Durack accepted she was, in fact, the highly praised indigenous painter Eddie Burrup. Her daughter had seen her paintings and said, 'If these were done by an Aboriginal they would get somewhere.' Later they had taken a walk together and standing under a tree Elizabeth had said, 'I'm not totally opposed to signing these morphological works under a nom-de-plume.' And so 'Eddie' was born.

MORE RECENTLY Norma Khomi's *Forbidden Love*, a novel of persecution of women in Jordan, was withdrawn from the Australian bookshelves in 2004. The novel tells of the honour killing of her friend, Dalia, whose crime was to fall in love with Michael, a Christian army officer, and of being forced to flee from Jordan to Australia after she confronted her dead friend's family. It was an enormous success in Australia and the media decided that she was a symbol of both women's rights and religious tolerance. However, the media was embarrassed once it realised that Ms Khomi had left Jordan as a young child and had married and lived in Chicago until 2000.

JOHN DREWE commissioned up to 200 faked paintings at £250 a time during his 12-year spell of selling forged works by modern masters such as Ben Nicholson, Chagal, Giacometti and Graham Sutherland. Drewe, who claimed to have a PhD in physics, answered an advertisement in *Private Eye*, placed by the impoverished artist John

Myatt who offered genuine 'fakes' at £150 a painting. Drewe, born John Crockett, increased the fee, and gained access to the archives of the Tate as well as the Victoria and Albert Museum where he doctored the records, inserting photographs of Myatt's paintings. Myatt's fakes were painted using a mixture of emulsion and K-Y jelly and were aged with vacuum-cleaner dust. Fifteen fakes were sold through Sotheby's, Christie's and Phillips' – one 'Ben Nicholson' fetched £107,000.

The end came when Drewe's wife, Batsheva Goudsmid, now in the middle of an acrimonious divorce, found various papers left by Drewe and went to the police. In February 1999 Drewe was sentenced to six years in prison and Myatt, who gave evidence for the prosecution, to a year. At that time there were up to 140 paintings still untraced. In January 2006 St Paul's Gallery in Birmingham held an exhibition of Myatt's 'genuine fakes'. He can now command between £1,000 and £10,000 a picture.

Not too many a conman is given the opportunity to prove he was not a collaborator during the Second World War. Han van Meegeren, the Dutch forger, principally of Vermeers, was give three weeks to create a fake to prove that his earlier painting *Christ with the Adultress*, which had been obtained by Reichmarshall Hermann Goering, was also a fake.

Van Meegeren was born in Holland in 1889. When he rejected modern art, and in turn collectors rejected his paintings in the styles of earlier centuries, he took to faking Old Masters not only as a means of earning a living but also to expose the so-called experts, in particular the Dutch authority on Vermeer, Dr Abraham Bredius.

It took him several years to complete *Christ and the Disciples at Emmaus* and when he had comprehensively deceived Bredius he nearly fessed up, but instead, having sold the painting for what would now be millions of pounds, he began another and another.

In the seven years from 1938 he painted a further six Vermeers as well as some Frans Hals and Pieter de Hoochs. In 1942 one of his Vermeers sold for 1,600,000 guilders. It was the last of the batch, *Christ with the Adultress*, which caused the trouble when it was found in an Austrian salt mine and traced back to van Meegeren. He was arrested and charged with collaboration. His defence was that it was a fake and that, since Goering had handed over a number of genuine paintings in exchange for the work, he was a hero rather than villain.

Now under house arrest, the authorities asked him to produce a copy of one of his fakes but instead, in three weeks, he painted the last van Meegeren, *The Young Christ Teaching in the Temple*. Van Meegeren told a committee of experts what paintings they would find underneath the supposed Vermeers and the charge was changed to forgery.

Sentenced to two years, van Meegeren had a heart attack and never went to prison. Instead he died in a clinic on 29 December 1947. In all he made more than 7 million guilders from his paintings, equivalent to about $2 million then and roughly about 20 times that amount in today's money.

Born in 1752 Thomas Chatterton passed off a number of poems and prose works as those of a fifteenth-century monk and mediaeval imaginary writer, Thomas Rowley. They were initially hailed as a magnificent find by the local literati, but Chatterton was soon exposed as the true author and decided to come to London to seek his fortune as a poet. He failed to find a patron and, on the point of starvation, committed suicide by swallowing arsenic at the age of 17. He later became a hero of the romantic poets, including Keats and Coleridge who composed works about him. Today, he is best remembered for the 1856 pre-Raphaelite painting *The Death of Chatterton* by Henry Wallis.

In 1898 Louis de Rougemont sold the amazing story of his adventures to *World Wide* magazine. He had been shipwrecked somewhere near the Australian mainland, something only he and the ship's dog, which had valiantly dragged him through the waves, survived. They lived on a 100-yard-long island for two years during which time he built a house, managed to light a fire which he kept going and raised corn. Two years later two Aborigines arrived on the island and, having built a boat together, they all sailed for the mainland, where he went native and married Yamba.

His amazing adventures continued. Alligators were wrestled, emus shot and eaten, battles fought with the losing tribesmen being eaten themselves. Later Yamba ate her child to leave the only available food for Rougemont when he was taken ill. He cured himself by burrowing into the carcass of a dead buffalo. Then he decided to return to England, sadly without the gallant Yamba, who had taken to wearing the bones of her dead child around her neck. His story was an amazing success.

It was the *Daily Chronicle* that challenged Rougemont to prove his story and, of course, he could not do so. He was, in fact, the

Swiss-born Henri Louis Grien who had run away from home at the age of 16 and been taken up by the fading actress Fanny Kemble who took him on her theatrical tours. He tried his hand at a number of jobs including street photographer, selling mining shares, dishwasher and restaurant waiter, as well as working as a butler to Sir William Robinson, Governor of Western Australia. All the information for his story had come from the diaries of a man who had left them behind in a Sydney restaurant, supplemented by research at the British Museum.

For a time Grien became a music-hall turn, riding turtles in a tank on the stage of the London Hippodrome in Leicester Square, but by the time of his death he had been reduced to selling matches in Piccadilly.

ONE OF THE problems for the young violinist Fritz Kreisler in late nineteenth-century Vienna was the lack of repertory available to him. Bach was out of fashion and the sonatas of Beethoven demanded a high degree of technical ability by the accompanist. To meet the problem he began to compose pieces supposedly by little-known or forgotten masters such as Couperin and Pugnani. These he 'discovered' in libraries during his travels. Of course there was disagreement among his critics. Some thought the pieces worthy of Bach while one wrote of his playing, 'naturally his temperament lacks the strength and maturity to reach the heights of Pugnani'. Then Kreisler produced and performed some 'posthumous' waltzes by Joseph Lanner, a contemporary of Johann Strauss the Elder. When the critic of the *Berliner Tageblatt* complained that Kreisler had dared to perform his own *Caprice Viennoise* in the same set as these masterpieces which were worthy of Schubert, Kreisler wrote admitting they were all composed by him. No one took any notice and it was not until his sixtieth birthday in 1935 that, on being asked point blank if he had written so much of his repertory, he admitted that indeed he had.

The admission brought heavy criticism, but this was something he wore lightly. He was defended by the *Philadelphia Record*:

> In the first place, no one would have wanted to hear the pieces if they had been ascribed to the then unknown Kreisler. In the second place, no one would have bought them. In the third place, rival players would not have put them on their own programme if they had known who the composer really was.

AFTER JOYCE Hatto, the English concert pianist, was diagnosed as having cancer in the 1970s, she never performed in public again. She did, however, undertake a series of recordings in a studio at her home in Hertfordshire of the music of a wide range of composers from Haydn and Brahms to Bax and Bliss. In 2007 an analysis of her recordings of works by Liszt, Rachmaninov and Godowsky were found to be identical to those of other pianists. Others were soon to follow. In March 2007, her husband admitted that he had included recordings by other artistes in his wife's work.

JEAN DE SPERATI, arguably the greatest philatelic faker of all time, was born in Pisa, Italy, in 1884 but lived most of his life in France. He first started making forgeries in 1910 by buying inexpensive old stamps, bleaching out the images and replacing them with exact copies of rare stamps. Because they had authentic watermarks and perforations on the correct period paper, the stamps looked completely genuine.

He ran into trouble in 1942 when French Customs seized a package he was sending to a dealer in Lisbon. Confessing that he had been a successful stamp forger for 30 years, in order to avoid a huge fine for exporting valuable rare stamps, he proved they were forgeries – and therefore worthless – by making another identical set. On this occasion he was acquitted, but 20 years later he was charged again and sentenced to two years' imprisonment which, because of his age, he was not required to serve.

He is known to have forged some 566 stamps from more than 100 countries. They have become so collectible that now some, such as the red 1913 Australian £2 stamp, are worth more than the originals he copied.

In 1954 at the age of 70 with his eyesight failing, the British Philatelic Association bought up Sperati's entire stock and produced a definitive reference book of his work. However, when he died three years later, it was discovered he had still been hard at work. 'Just for fun,' he confided shortly before his death.

In 1970 shortly after the publication of *Fake!* – Clifford Irving's biography of the art forger Elmyr de Hory – he and his friend Dick Suskind decided, as a joke, to write the 'authorised' biography of the reclusive billionaire Howard Hughes. The magnate, who had made his money in engineering and who had promoted the sex siren Jane Russell, was then living on the top floor of the Desert Inn, Las Vegas, running his empire by telephone. He had not been seen in the outside world for 15 years.

The proposal was put to the publishers McGraw-Hill, but of course Hughes would only communicate with them through Irving. Using a photograph of Hughes's handwriting as a key and a pad of the sort of legal paper he knew Hughes used, Irving wrote letters to the publishers saying, 'It would not suit me to die without having certain misconceptions of my life cleared up ... .' McGraw-Hill agreed to pay $100,000 on signing the contract to write the book, $100,000 on delivery of a transcript of the interviews and $300,000 for the manuscript. Irving's wife Edith opened a Swiss bank account in the name Helga Hughes and one in the name Hanne Rosencrantz.

Irving then obtained the files of *Life* magazine, and from them he and Suskind put together tape-recorded interviews. When a rival biography was mooted, Irving, posing as Hughes, telegraphed Mc-Graw-Hill to say he had heard of an offer of $250,000 for the serial rights and wanted another $1 million.

The transcript was duly delivered and the advance was raised to $750,000. Irving was put through a lie-detector test and passed. Later McGraw-Hill commissioned a handwriting expert to confirm the authenticity of the letters Irving was writing as Hughes, which he did.

On 7 December 1971 the publishers announced the forthcoming publication and, after Hughes denounced the book through his lawyers, further handwriting experts again confirmed the Irving letters as genuine. Shortly after Christmas the recluse gave his first interview in a decade and a half when, speaking over the telephone, he denied he had ever met Irving. Irving responded saying the voice over the line had not been that of Hughes. But the game was up. Detectives traced the bank accounts and another writer saw the manuscript and recognised that some of the stories came from his own unpublished work.

Irving was sentenced to 30 months in jail, Suskind six and Edith fared the worst. Not only did she serve two months of a two-year sentence in the US, but she also served a two-year intermittent sentence in Zurich. After his release Irving, with Suskind, wrote *Project Octavio*, an account of the hoax. He then took to writing best-selling crime thrillers. Hughes apparently died on 5 April 1976 while flying on a private Lear jet from Acapulco to Houston. Irving is listed as giving technical advice for a film starring Richard Gere being made about the scam.

WHEN THE author A.N.Wilson, then writing a biography of John Betjeman, received a letter from an Eve de Harben enclosing what purported to be a copy of one written by the former poet laureate to a mistress, he was delighted. Betjeman had often complained that he had not had enough sex in his lifetime and here was a hitherto unrevealed episode. The letter was duly included in the book published in 2006.

Unfortunately it was then pointed out that the first letter of each sentence of the supposed love letter spelled out 'A.N. WILSON IS A SHIT'. Suspicion fell on Bevis Hillier – the letter had been posted in his home town of Winchester – another biographer of Betjeman whose earlier book had been cruelly reviewed by Wilson. Hillier, after first denying involvement, later admitted the hoax.

Peter 'Ringer' Barrie

EVEN WITH THE wind in its favour, the racehorse Coat of Mail, trained by jockey Jack Leach's father, was best described as moderate and in September 1919 it was sold for export. A month later it won a two-year-old race at Stockton. When Jack Leach spoke to the winning jockey, Billy Griggs, he was told it was the best two-year-old he had ever ridden. That was not surprising since it was the four-year-old Jazz, which had been third in the Flying Handicap at Newmarket the year before, rung in for the two-year-old. The coup had been arranged by Peter 'Ringer' Barrie and the horses looked nothing like each other. Afterwards people walked up to him saying, 'That's a nice coat of mail but you've had it dyed.'

Barrie had been running and doping horses for some years before he perfected his schemes. Before Coat of Mail he had proposed to run his three-year-old Mexican Belle as a two-year-old at Doncaster in a seller (where the winner is immediately sold at public auction), and then run her in another two days later. She was both dyed and doped and, reacting badly to the drugs, raced out of control and finished last.

Arrested over the Coat of Mail switch, he pleaded guilty and received three years. After his release Barrie went to Canada and, bribing his way across the border, went to New York. For the next decade he ran a string of ringers in the US. During his time there he is said to have cleared over $8 million including over $1 million when, in October 1931, he substituted Aknahton for the indifferent but appropriately named Sham, which won at 52-1 at Havre de Grace in Maryland. Throughout, Barrie was heavily involved with the prohibition mobs and gamblers in Chicago and New York. Arrested in 1934 over a bad cheque, the Grand Jury declined to indict him and instead he was deported.

Some papers claimed Barrie died in 1935 worn out by his efforts trying to avoid the Pinkerton Detective Agency and Scotland Yard. In fact, back in England, he was running a racing tipping sheet in 1939 and was warned off a British racecourse in 1945. He died on 6 July 1973 at the age of 85 in the Greenwich District Hospital. He had been living in a council home for single men.

All bets are off

O F THE MANY racing swindles, and there have indeed been many, one of the greatest ever must be that of the Trodmore Races, never run in August 1898. It was a coup that was thought to have netted something in the region of £250,000 and it would have been considerably more had it not been for a printer's error. In those days many small jumping and flat meetings were held on August Bank Holiday and the editor of the *Sportsman* received a press release announcing the first running of Trodmore Races in Cornwall on the Bank Holiday. No doubt the paper would wish to cover the meeting and report on the betting. No doubt it would, but there was the problem of staff.

The question was solved when an English sporting gent arrived unannounced in the editor's offices and offered to report on the meeting. Runners and riders were provided with possible odds and there was heavy betting. At the end of the day the correspondent, 'G. Martin', wired in the results and starting prices with one horse, Reaper, having won at 5-2. *Sporting Life*, not wishing to be outdone, then reprinted the results and this time the odds of Reaper were mistakenly given as 5-1. A bookmaker wishing to know the correct odds made enquiries, but of G. Martin there was no trace. There was no registered horse named Reaper and, worst of all, there was no place named Trodmore. The perpetrators, suspected to be a group of journalists, were never caught. In an article on 2 August 1998 commemorating the centenary of the coup, the *Racing Post* wondered just how many previous Trodmores there had been.

O NE OF THE great switches at a racetrack came on 16 July 1953 when, as jockey Billy Gilchrist said afterwards, 'I picked up the stick, gave him one and he went right away to win by two lengths.' The 'him' was Fracasal running at 10-1 in the Bath Selling Plate. Except it was not Fracasal but a smart French horse, Santa Amaro, running in place of the very moderate plater (a poor-class racehorse).

There had been very heavy betting on the horse all over the country and in pre-computer days normally when this happened the money was 'blown back' by a special telephone on to the track and so the starting price was reduced. That afternoon the blower wires had been cut and so the bookmakers could not hedge their bets. Harry Kateley, the leader of the coup which should have netted a minimum of £60,000, instead received three years. Poor Billy Gilchrist did not even receive his riding fee.

Derby Day 1933 saw one of the greatest racing welshing coups of the decade. A motor lorry was hired for 30 shillings and a portable totalisator was constructed with a display of flags, posters and banners. There were three separate windows of 5 shillings, 10 shillings and £1 and the operators wore clean linen coats and tinted glasses. It was set up next to the St Dustan's Derby Day section and took bets only on the big race, attracting such a crowd that the police arrived to help control the queues. When the 'Off' was sounded the crowd went to watch the race and during the five minutes available to them the tricksters dismantled the tote and disappeared. It is said the gang cleared £1,600.

· 172 ·

Not exactly a con, but certainly a great coup, was the running of Lord George Bentinck's horse Elis in the 1836 running of the St Leger. In those days, horses had to be walked to the various race-courses, so when bookmakers discovered that Elis was still down in Goodwood just a few days before the Doncaster race, the odds were duly lengthened. However, what the bookies hadn't reckoned on was Bentinck devising the first horse transporter. A specially constructed horse-drawn carriage took Elis to Doncaster in time for the race. The horse romped home, having been sent off the 7-2 second favourite, making Lord George a fortune in the process.

The crooked financier Horatio Bottomley was said to have been involved in a race swindle at Blankenberg in Belgium. He had all six horses in one race and, with bets down, had paid the jockeys to finish in a certain order. Unfortunately, shortly before the race a sea mist blew up and the jockeys, who could not see or even hear each other, finished in the wrong order.

First past the post in the 1844 Derby was Maccabeus, racing under the name of Running Rein, a four-year-old in a race for three-year-old colts. The fraud was worked by a gambler, Goodman Levy, who ran the horse in the name of an Epsom corn merchant. There had been a failed objection to the horse when it won as a 'two'-year-old. Now it was decided that before the race there would be an examination of its mouth – a horse's age can be told from its teeth – and if it won, an objection could be lodged.

The favourite, Ugly Buck, was ridden foul and the second favourite, Ratan, was not only 'got at' the night before but was pulled by his jockey. While leading the race, the German-owned Leander was brought down and was later destroyed. An examination of its mouth showed it to be a four-year-old. Running Rein won by three quarters of a length but, as its mouth examination had confirmed it as a four-year-old, the race was awarded to Orlando, owned by Colonel Peel, the brother of the Prime Minister, Sir Robert.

Running Rein or Maccabeus disappeared and Goodman, who stood to win £50,000 over the coup, fled the country. The judge at a subsequent trial over payment of the winnings commented, 'If gentlemen condescended to race with blackguards, they must condescend to be cheated.'

RINGING HORSES continues. On August Bank Holiday 1978 trainer and former amateur jockey John Bowles ran talented Cobbler's March as the appropriately named In the Money before the scam was discovered after winning a seller at 8-1 at Newton Abbott. He was given a suspended prison sentence and warned off for 20 years. In 1998 he was given a licence to train in Ireland.

ON 29 MARCH 1982 businessman Ken Richardson's three-year-old horse Good Hand, running as the two-year-old Flockton Grey and ridden by an unknowing Kevin Darley, won a maiden race at Leicester by 20 lengths. Richardson received a suspended sentence and turned his attention to football clubs. First he took over Bridlington, which soon went into receivership, after which he turned his attention to the unfortunate Doncaster Rovers. His association with the club ended when he was sentenced to four years' imprisonment in 1998 after arranging for the club's stand to be burned down.

ON 11 JUNE 1998 Bold Faith was given what was described as a 'fine ride' in an amateur's race at Newbury by Mr A. Jacobs, a 29-year-old Puerto Rican. It was his first winner in Britain and it was not his last. On 24 June he gave another good display on George Dillingham at Carlisle. The press began to talk about him and he shyly admitted that whereas his family was not involved in racing his godfather was the celebrated jockey Angel Cordero Jnr. Indeed, he told some people he had been orphaned at birth and the nurses had named him Angel because of his sweet temperament.

He was far too good a jockey to have come from nowhere. After his fifth win in 21 races, this time at Beverley on Gymcrack Flyer on 13 August, he posed for photographs which were sent to the Amateur Riders' Club of America. There the happy jockey was identified as the professional Angel Monserrate, who had been banned in 1995 after failing a drugs test. Riding as Carlos Castro, whose credit cards and identity he had stolen when they shared a room, he had also ridden a winner at Aqueduct, New York, in November 1996. In November 1998 the Jockey Club banned him for ten years. By this time he was working in a restaurant in Cambridge. Cordero Jnr said it was the first he knew about having Jacobs as a godson. One of Jacobs's friends remarked, 'I expect he will come back to ride in a ladies' race under the name Gloria Estefan.'

1998 WAS A GOOD year for 'rung-in' jockeys. That year the former Scottish apprentice Colin Campbell was deported from Canada where he had also ridden five winners as Gary Cruse. In December the Mexican apprentice Fernando Velasquez, who had ridden over 60 winners in Washington State, turned out to be the seasoned professional Cuevas Cuellar.

NOT ALL RACING coups work out and sometimes the consequences are fatal for those who let the side down. The body of Australian racehorse trainer George Brown, who had ridden over jumps in England, was found tortured and murdered in a burned-out car on the F6 Freeway in Australia, in April 1984. Brown, it seems, had agreed to participate in the ring-in of his filly Risley at Doomben on 31 March and had then backed out. The last-minute presentation of Risley's papers cost him an AU$50 fine. His failure to go through with the switch cost those who had backed her down from 12-1 to 6-1 their money, and him his life.

In some ways, the running of Gay Future in 1974 at Cartmel, the small National Hunt course in the Lake District, was a classic betting coup. An Irish millionaire, Tony Murphy, sent his smart horse, Gay Future, over to a small Scottish-based trainer, Tony Collins, who trained it to peak fitness. However, in its place, another, poor-quality animal was put on view to the press. When Gay Future ran at the August Bank Holiday meeting it started at 10-1, helped by soap powder being rubbed into its legs to suggest sweating and with an able, but relatively unknown amateur Irish jockey on board. A winner by 15 lengths, the horse was backed in doubles and trebles with two other horses from Collins' stables, neither of which reached the courses at which they were entered. As a result all the money went on single bets on Gay Future. In fact neither of the other horses had left the stable.

The large amount of Irish bets on the horse, which would have produced in today's money something approaching £3 million, led to an investigation. Bookmakers refused to pay out, and for a time Special Branch were investigating.

Murphy came back to England on trial for conspiracy to defraud; both he and Collins were fined £1,000. The judge, Mr Justice Caulfield, told him it would be absurd to regard him as a fraudulent man and added that Collins had 'very fine qualities'. Both men, however, were warned off for ten years. A stable lad who failed to appear for the prosecution was given a month's imprisonment. Back in Ireland Murphy became a hero and *Murphy's Stroke*, a film about the coup, starred Pierce Brosnan.

'Bludger Bill' Warren

AN EARLY AUSTRALIAN conman working the London scene was William Charles 'Bludger Bill' Warren. (Bludger is the name given in Australia to men who live off immoral earnings.) Born in 1868 he was first convicted at Sydney Quarter Sessions on 12 February 1901. In England he worked a variety of confidence tricks, including taking money to bet on horse racing. He would promptly disappear with the cash and, when found, would either say, quite correctly that the horse had lost, or, if it had won, plead a defence under the Gaming Acts, which made gambling debts irrecoverable at law. In this way, in 1912, posing as Mr Fairie, owner of the Ascot Gold Cup winner Aleppo, he cleared £12,000.

The end of this particular trick came in 1921 when a bookmaker was awarded £15,000 against Warren on the grounds that he had fraudulently obtained the money. A great number of other actions were pending and when his Australian friends Robert Bradshaw, Charles McNally and Alfred Dean were arrested over a game of Anzac Poker, Warren disappeared. Between them, McNally and Dean were said to have cleared over £90,000 in crooked card games and racecourse swindles. They each received five years at the Central Criminal Court.

Warren prudently went to Brussels and then France, setting up home on the Riviera. Before he left, there had been a number of other coups in London including the defrauding of a Jamaican plantation owner. He had set up home with a woman confidence trickster named Dora who posed as his wife, and the pair obtained loans from money lenders and had been buying goods on extended credit. There was also the Badger Game and crooked poker to be played. Left behind, Dora received 18 months' imprisonment.

In early 1923 two Australians were arrested in Paris after relieving an American of 4,000 francs. In April that year Warren drove from

Monte Carlo to Paris to try to assist them and was promptly arrested at the Porte d'Orleans, suspected of being the head of a gang of international swindlers. He claimed mistaken identity but an Englishman was brought to Paris and picked him out as having swindled him out of £23,000 over a race at Longchamps. When he was arrested Warren was said to have a staggering £800,000 in cash and jewellery hidden in his Rolls-Royce. He received five years but, released early, he was in America in 1927 working another racing swindle.

He was regarded as still active in 1947 when he was listed in Scotland Yard's directory of international confidence tricksters.

This unsporting life

EVEN IN THE DAYS when sport was more or less wholly amateur, there were some notable cons worked. Among them was that of Rosie Ruiz, who won the 1980 Boston marathon on 21 April 1980, after she had qualified by finishing in the New York 1979 version of the event. Unfortunately there seemed to have been no sighting of her on the video footage of her coming through the field earlier in the race. Instead spectators reported she had jumped out of the crowd in the last mile to win in a canter by three minutes. As for the New York race, there were reports that she had taken the subway. She was disqualified but refused to return her first-place medal. The race was awarded to Jacqueline Gareau from Montreal who was given a larger version of the medal.

ELEVEN YEARS later, the 1991 Brussels marathon was won by the Algerian runner Abbes Tehami. Sadly for him it was noticed that he had begun the race with a moustache and ended it without one. Since there were no shaving facilities provided at the water stations, enquiries were made which showed that the No. 62 bib had been worn at the start by Bensalem Hamiami, Tehami's coach. Seven and a half miles down the course Hamiami ran into the woods and Tehami emerged wearing the bib. It had been noticed that at the time Hamiami ran off the course he was tiring but Tehami caught up with the leaders three miles later and ran on strongly. Neither stayed for the medal ceremony and the race went to the Soviet runner Anatoly Karipanov.

TEHAMI AND RUIZ come from a long, if not honourable, tradition. During the World Fair of 1893 a horse race was organised from the Baline Hotel in Chadron, Nebraska to finish at Buffalo Bill Cody's Wild West arena in Chicago. The winner was to receive a prize of $1,500 and a saddle. Each man could have two horses, one of which could be changed, but he had to be riding one of the starting horses at the finish. The winner was John Berry who, after 14 days in the saddle, rode into Chicago at 9.30 a.m. on 27 June where he was greeted by Buffalo Bill himself and a crowd of 10,000. Although he got the saddle he did not receive the cash. It was discovered that soon after the start he had loaded his horses on to a train, covering the first hundred miles in both more comfort and a quicker time than his rivals.

FINALLY ON the subject of marathon runners, in 1994 a Nottinghamshire man was forced to give up work after sustaining a back injury. He was unable to walk more than 55 yards in five minutes and needed help with feeding and any outdoor activity. From 2001 he was paid over £22,000 in state benefits, but, by that year he had recovered so well that he was running for Sutton Harriers in 10 kilometre races. While still receiving benefits in 2004 he completed the London marathon in 3 hours 35 minutes. In January 2006 he admitted failing to notify a change in his circumstances and was jailed for ten months.

A SPORT IN which the upper-class victim could be plucked was, appropriately enough, pigeon shooting, at which the crooked jockey Tod Sloan excelled. In 1903 Robert Sievier – gambler, man about town and owner of the wonderful filly Sceptre – was sued over a stopped cheque for £4,000 which he had dropped betting on a pigeon shoot in Monte Carlo in the spring of 1901. He claimed he was not liable in law as it was a gambling debt but was also keen to tell the court why he had stopped the cheque. He had been betting on a man, Baratz, who, he claimed, when he called 'pull' and a 'very tame pigeon came hovering out of the trap', shot three yards below it. When the bird settled six yards from him on the mat and, under the rules, he was entitled to kill it, he failed to do so. There was also a suggestion Baratz was firing blanks. Sievier claimed he had only issued the cheque because he was warned that when Sceptre was running in Paris she would be 'got at'. She ran unharmed and he stopped the cheque forthwith. Judgment to Sievier.

Aᴌɪ Dɪᴀ managed to play 53 minutes for Southampton FC on 21 November 1996. He was recommended to Graeme Souness, the club's manager, as a Senegalese international who had played for Paris St Germain. In fact he had failed a trial for Rotherham United. He was signed on a month's trial by Southampton and on his only outing for the club appeared as a substitute against Leeds United and was himself substituted. He is generally regarded as the worst player the club ever had. A Southampton supporters' chant went 'Ali Dia is a liar'.

Iɴ ɴɪɴᴇᴛᴇᴇɴᴛʜ-ᴄᴇɴᴛᴜʀʏ America one of the favourite cons when pedestrianism was at its height was the fixed foot race, although foot racing itself was illegal. The apparent secretary of a millionaire keen on the sport would approach a dupe and offer to double-cross his employer by fixing the race and sharing the profits with the victim after the mark had put up the betting money himself. The likely winner would collapse during the race and sometimes a 'doctor' would even announce his death. In the confusion the secretary would disappear with the victim's stake.

The greatest exponent of the con was William Elmer Mead, who ran these races in small towns where he had bribed the local sheriff, first to allow the race and then to arrest the gamblers. Acting as stakeholder, Mead would be the one who first saw the approaching sheriff and head the run towards the station to put the dupe on board a train with the promise to meet up in the next town. His refinement was to send a telegram announcing the death of the runner. Eventually the con became so well known that it was time to move to new pastures such as fixing horse racing.

ANZAC POKER was the name of the game with which Australian conmen regularly trapped their European victims in the 1920s. All the players put an agreed sum in the pool and the dealer turned up a card. He then bet the whole or part of the pool that the next card turned up would be higher than the one exposed. If he won then he took the whole or part of the pool and the cards passed to the player on his left. Aces were low. The trick was that two packs were used and the first was switched after three Aces were exposed. On turning a two, the mark, believing he effectively could not lose, then bet a substantial amount and was dismayed to find the fourth Ace turn up.

AT A SOUTHEND greyhound track in 1949 Red Wind won an Open puppy race over 500 yards in less time than it had taken to cover 460 yards in a trial four days earlier. It had been backed to win £4,000. A check of its details tallied but enquiries in Ireland showed the owner had bought a dog named Waggles. When the former trainer's wife came over to England and went to see 'Red Wind', Waggles recognised her at once. In July 1950 the owner and his brother were convicted at the Old Bailey and received up to two years' imprisonment. Dogs had been switched at two other tracks.

THERE WAS ONE spectacular and nearly successful effort at fixing the odds when, on 30 June 1964, the sixth race at Dagenham greyhounds was the 4.05 p.m. Open over 840 yards flat. Seven tote booths and every tote window taking forecast bets were blocked by men placing a series of bets. By backing 18 out of 30 combinations the conspirators fed money into a pool by making certain losing bets. The other 12 combinations were backed to one unit on each. The odds produced were phenomenal and one punter, John Turner, claimed £987 on a two-shilling bet. The winning odds of the second and third favourites, Buck Wheat and Handsome Lass, coming first and second were 10,000-1. The favourite was third so this effectively eliminated any doping allegations. It was claimed that the stadium should have refused to declare a dividend on the race.

Next day Turner told how he had masterminded the coup with 125 helpers each paid £5 with a bonus of between £50 and £100 if it was successful. He had borrowed £3,500 as a stake. The bookmakers screamed in agony saying they would not pay and the debts were not legally enforceable. The National Association of Bookmakers and The National Sporting League issued a statement that the race was void and the correct conduct was to refund the stakes.

John Turner, along with two other men, was prosecuted for conspiracy to defraud, but at the third hearing on 19 January 1966 the prosecution offered no evidence. The winnings, had they been paid, would have been between £7 million and £10 million.

Proven fixing in football matches is rare. In 1913 a man was imprisoned for five months for trying to bribe the English full back to ensure West Bromwich Albion lost to or drew with Everton.

Shortly before the Second World War there was an attempt by the former Scotland and Celtic player Archie 'Punch' Kyle to bribe Hamilton Academicals to lose an easy home match to Leith Athletic. He first approached the captain, Willie Moffatt, who promptly told the directors who told the police. A second meeting was arranged with a police officer hidden behind a curtain who recorded the conversation. Kyle received a short sentence. Hamilton played well that Saturday but still lost.

There is an unconfirmed story that, in the 1950s, the players of a Third Division (North) club put their week's wages on the opposition. Unfortunately they omitted to tell their new young, keen and talented centre forward who, after a solo run, equalised in the last minute.

Among sports fans, those who have followed professional wrestling have been the ones most often deceived. In the heyday of the 1970s, when a bout between Jackie Pallo and Mick McManus televised just before the Cup Final would draw an audience of millions, small promoters around the country would put on bouts advertised as Pallo v. McManus. It was only when the wrestlers entered the ring that the punters realised they were watching Syd (or Tommy, etc.) Pallo and Bill (or Harry, etc.) McManus. There were also a number of wrestlers to be unmasked, the most popular of which was 'Dr Death', of whom there were also a number. Generally speaking, in the South, Dr Death was the promoter and deviser Paul Lincoln, while in the North it was Ted Beech, who often appeared as himself on the first half of the bill before donning the mask.

Occasionally the fans were goaded beyond endurance. In 1968 at a tournament in Grimsby the promoter was attacked and had to be rescued from the spectators by the police and dogs. The cause of discontent was the failure of half the main event to appear, compounded by a wrestler on the first half of the bill being pressed into service in the second to make up numbers. The final straw was that the cognoscenti realised that the 'Red Devil' was obviously an impostor.

ONE OF THE great automata of the nineteenth century was 'The Turk', a supposedly mechanical chess player that could beat any human. Made out of wood and dressed in a turban and bejewelled robes, it was the invention of a Hungarian engineer Wolfgang von Kempelen. The figure was seated at a chessboard and in the spring of 1780 a challenge at the court of the Empress Marie Theresa was made to any member of the audience who cared to play it. Von Kempelen produced a key, wound up The Turk and play commenced. The machine is reported to have beaten a Count Cobenzl in half an hour.

Von Kempelen became bored with his invention and it was not until 1781 that The Turk was wheeled out again to perform at the state visit of Grand Duke Paul of Russia. The next spring von Kempelen took him to Paris, where he defeated the US statesman Benjamin Franklin at the Café de la Régence. In turn The Turk was defeated by the great French chess master François-André Philidor. The Turk came to England in 1793 and is credited with inspiring Edward Cartwright to invent the power loom. After a tour of Germany and Holland, The Turk once again retired.

It was only after von Kempelen's death that his son sold The Turk

to the Austrian showman Johann Nepomuk Maelzel for 10,000 francs. Now The Turk played Napoleon in Vienna in 1809, toured England and the US, passing through various hands until, on 5 July 1854, he perished in a fire at the Chinese Museum in Philadelphia.

From the start there were rival theories of how the machine worked, or rather how the trick was done. These included: using a child, a midget, a limbless ex-serviceman and even a chess-playing monkey; or, that it was done by magnetism or by pulling strings. Then in 1821, Robert Willis, after studying The Turk, wrote a treatise explaining that an adult could, in fact, fit inside the figure. Fifteen years later Edgar Allen Poe came to the same conclusion and added that the brains of The Turk, at the time, were those of the talented chess player William Schlumberger, who had been spotted in the late 1820s climbing out of the machine. Fortunately, at the time it had been passed off as a publicity stunt. It is thought that over the years some 15 players were The Turk. The man who defeated Napoleon was the Viennese master, Johann Allgaier.

Guillermo Rosales

IN 1993 GUILLERMO Rosales first landed on his feet when he fell from the undercarriage of a DC8 airliner on to the runway of Miami airport. At the age of 13 this orphan had managed to cling to the plane on a three-hour flight from Bogota, Colombia. He was taken to a McDonald's for his first symbolic meal on American soil and was later adopted by a Miami detective and his wife. This is the stuff American dreams are made of. Except that he was not an orphan; he was 17 and his real name was Juan Carlos Guzman-Betancourt. He stole from the detective and his wife, and there have been subsequent doubts about the whole story of his flight. Over the next 12 years, as an Arabian billionaire, a priest, a German, a waiter, a rich tourist, an airline employee and another dozen identities, he went on to become one of the world's great twenty-first-century conmen. He specialised in hotel burglaries, modelling himself on Raffles, the fictional jewel thief.

He was deported from the US after stealing from the detective and his wife but he was back in New York within the month. After that he went to Miami and in 1997 was again deported. In 1998 he was in London stealing from guests at Le Meridien Hotel. He paid a fine and was off before his identity was discovered. He then operated in France, Russia, Japan and North America, before he was again arrested in London in 2004 and jailed for three years. He was gone within three months; he was detained in an open prison on the Isle of Sheppey in Kent and, allowed out for a visit to the dentist, he never returned.

A talented linguist, his stock in trade has been to hang around lobbies of the world's great hotels exchanging money with the cashiers, ingratiating himself with the other staff and generally picking up information about who was staying in which room by looking at discarded bar bills and health-club bookings. He would then approach the front desk saying he had lost his key and be given a duplicate. Once in a guest's room he would, correctly, say he could not open the room safe, could someone please come and change the lock for him? And, time and again, they did.

He was jailed for two years in Dublin in 2006 for theft from guests at the Merrion Hotel and subsequent credit-card offences. The authorities in France, Britain and the US also wished to see him.

Deadly cons

ON 24 NOVEMBER 1974 the Labour MP for Walsall, Privy Councillor John Stonehouse, disappeared from his hotel on Miami Beach. His clothes were found neatly folded on the veranda along with his passport. He had financial troubles and was being investigated by the Department of Trade and Industry. Initially it was presumed he had drowned himself, but on Christmas Eve that year he was found living under the name Donald Muldoon in St Kilda, a beachside suburb of Melbourne, by police who were actually looking for the also-vanished Lord Lucan. Having obtained a forged passport in the name of one of his constituents, Stonehouse had gone to Australia to begin a new life with his mistress.

There were problems with his extradition and he tried to obtain asylum from both Mauritius and Sweden, but he was finally deported back to the UK in August 1976 and received seven years at the Old Bailey for fraud. He was released in 1979 after suffering three heart attacks. He married his mistress in 1981, wrote a number of books and joined the now defunct Social Democrat Party. He died on 14 April 1988 after yet another heart attack.

In JUNE 2004 24-year-old Clayton Daniels was found dead behind the wheel of a burned-out Chevrolet at the bottom of a cliff near Georgetown, Texas. The fire had been so fierce that the body was unrecognisable, its head and limbs burned away. He had been due to surrender for a 30-day prison sentence for a sexual-assault offence committed when he was a teenager. His wife, Molly, arranged a memorial service and her co-workers put up $1,000 towards the cost. She soon had a new boyfriend, Jake, who, apart from his dyed black hair, indeed looked a good deal like the dead Clayton.

Insurance investigators, faced with a $100,000 claim, found that there were no skid marks or signs of a high-speed crash. The fire, helped by an accelerant, had begun in the driver's seat and DNA samples taken from the corpse did not match those taken from Clayton's mother. This was hardly surprising since the body was that of an 83-year-old woman who had died in 2003 and whose body Molly Daniels had exhumed. 'We felt because she was older there would not be much family upset', she told the court in May 2005 at her sentencing hearing. She received the maximum of 20 years after pleading guilty to insurance fraud and hindering apprehension.

In OCTOBER 2005 when Buttons, a three-year-old fox terrier which had been very ill for over a month with pancreatitis and a heart murmur, began vomiting, her owner James Kimberlin took her one last time to the Companion Animal Hospital in Collierville, Tennessee, to be put to sleep by veterinarian Jerry A. Truitt. The dog was given an injection, Truitt listened to her heart and told Kimberlin that Buttons had gone. A sympathy card was signed by Truitt and other members of the staff and sent to Kimberlin and his wife of 50 years, Betty Jody.

When Theresa Stewart, a veterinary technician at the hospital, who knew Buttons but had not been working on the day she was put down, returned to work, she was surprised to find the dog in a cage labelled Zipper and up for adoption. She said she wished to adopt her, took her to an outside veterinarian and when Zipper was confirmed as Buttons, put the dog on a no-fat diet and returned her to the Kimberlins. Truitt resigned from the hospital and offered to return the $1,000 fee. 'It's just all been a miracle, just a miracle', said Mrs Kimberlin.

In August 1897 Mary Laura, the wife of the conman Carl von Veltheim, identified a rope-bound naked body in the Thames near Wapping as her husband, probably to ward off any possible charges against him for his many bigamous marriages. Subsequently, she decided, quite correctly, that it was not he. Nearly a decade later there was another curious incident. On 10 March 1906 a woman named as Marie Derval died of poison in Liffen's Hotel, Pimlico. A Mrs Young came forward to say that the body was in fact that of Mary Laura who had been living in Cap Roquebrune with her nine-year-old son. It was generally regarded as a hoax.

In 1979 a member of the family of Johnny Sterling Martin called the Family Court in Columbia, South Carolina, to say he had died following a bar brawl in Alabama. Martin had escaped from a work gang some months earlier while serving a one-year sentence for failing to pay child support.

Following a tip-off by an ex-wife, Martin was arrested in January 2006 about 150 miles away in Myrtle Beach, where he had been living under his own name for about 20 years. Since his death he had remarried twice and had a third child. The maintenance arrears now totalled over $30,000. There was also a charge of escaping from custody to be faced.

On 17 August 2002 Dane Colson's bloodstained green Daewoo was discovered in a lane in Surry Hills, Sydney, after he had failed to return to work as a guard at Fox Studios. His pregnant fiancée reported him missing and the police feared he had been murdered. He resurfaced in South Australia in the December applying for benefits, surrendered himself to the police and then vanished again until, quite by chance, he was seen by a family member in Melbourne, Victoria. Arrested at the Royal Derby Hotel in Fitzroy, he was charged with an offence of public mischief and returned to New South Wales. It was not the first time he had faked his disappearance. He had done the same in 1997, for the same reason, when he discovered that a previous fiancée was pregnant. On that occasion he told the girl he had been abducted and held in the boot of a car.

When he was returned to Sydney, a new girlfriend came to give him moral support. She had met him when he was working as a body-piercing instructor in Adelaide. Indeed she had thought so highly of their relationship that she had made an appointment to have her tubes untied. On 3 April 2003 he was sentenced to 200 hours community service. The police reckoned the disappearance had cost them over AU$100,000.

It seems hard to kill off a son just to obtain time off work. But in 2005 in Waterloo, Iowa, Mary Jo Elizabeth Jensen, the mother of Dan 'D.J.' Reddout, and her boyfriend James Snyder did just that. They published Dan's obituary in the *Waterloo-Cedar Falls Courier* announcing his death after a short illness and that a graveside service had already taken place.

Jensen and Snyder had taken time off work before Christmas 2005 saying Dan was in hospital; sadly his condition deteriorated until he was placed on a life-support machine and died on Christmas Eve.

When the pair took more time off for mourning and their employers wanted more details of the boy's death, they provided a copy of the obituary as proof. It all came undone when all three of them were seen eating in a local restaurant some weeks after Dan's passing.

But they had nothing on Alfred James Chapman who, in 1916, told his London employers his son had died in hospital. His wife had also died and the money willed by her to her son had reverted to their eldest daughter, which had caused more expense. In turn, she had died of shock as a result of her mother's demise, and finally, his youngest daughter had died after hearing of the death of her soldier brother in Malta.

His employers were so distressed by the story that they purchased a wreath to be placed on Chapman's wife's grave. He took the flowers off and brought them home to the family saying they were table decorations from a dinner given by the firm. In August 1916 he received three months' hard labour at the Guildhall, London.

It is thought that in the US alone there are over 1,000 faked deaths a year. The motives can be trivial, such as that of the Des Moines, Iowa, woman Kimberly Du who faked her death in 2005 to avoid paying parking fines. She wrote her own obituary making it look like a page from the *Des Moines Register*'s website and sent a letter to the judge, apparently written by her mother, saying she had died in a car crash. The scheme unravelled when she was given another parking ticket a month after her death. In early 2006 she was given a two-year suspended sentence, put on probation and fined $500.

WHAT IOWA DID yesterday Wales does today. In February 2007 a Swansea woman pleaded guilty to attempting to pervert the course of justice by sending the Crown Prosecution Service a letter, purportedly from her daughter, to say she was dead. She had been trying to avoid a summons for speeding.

THE DEATHS may also be spur-of-the-moment cases, such as the man who took advantage of the October 1999 London Paddington rail crash in which 31 people died, to telephone the police casualty bureau to report himself missing. He had adopted a new name after his release from prison ten years earlier and took the opportunity, finally, to kill off his old self. It took the police a month and many hours of their time to uncover the deception. In 2000 he received a five-month sentence suspended for two years.

ONE OF THE more extraordinary defences in a murder case was run by Albertan Dr Abraham Cooper who claimed that Dr Ben Snider, with whom he had been quarrelling for some years, faked his own death to incriminate him. Cooper, who claimed that Snider had been conspiring to ruin his practice, had already filed a C$3.2 million claim against his rival. On 5 May 1999 Snider disappeared after telling his wife he was going to a meeting at Cooper's office. He was never seen again and his body never found but there were traces of blood on Cooper's clothes, office and car. In the autumn of 2000 Cooper was acquitted of murder but found guilty of Snider's manslaughter and was sentenced to seven years' and four months' imprisonment. Unusually in a manslaughter case the prosecution had asked for a sentence of life imprisonment.

IN CHICAGO IN 1900 model Mary Defenbach was persuaded by a detective Frank Brown, her lover, to take out insurance policies totalling $70,000 naming Frank Smilie, who pretended to be her fiancé and so had an insurable interest, as the beneficiary. Almost unbelievably she was also persuaded that she should allow herself to be 'killed' by a doctor August M. Unger. He would, she was told, give her a medicine which would induce a deathlike sleep. Once taken to the funeral home she would be revived and spirited away while the body of another woman would be cremated. She would be given half the proceeds.

All went according to plan so far as the conspirators were concerned, if not quite as Mary had envisaged things. On 25 August 1900 she died in agony. Unger signed the death certificate, an inquest was held with a bribed coroner and she was duly cremated.

Her uncle, however, was not satisfied and hired private investigators. One of the trio, Frank Smilie, turned state's evidence, but, because under state law of the time there could be no conviction without a body, Unger and Frank Brown could only be tried for fraud. Unger received five years; Brown was merely fined.

Editha Diss Debar

ONE OF THE CASES to shock (and entertain) *le tout* London in the autumn of 1901 was the trial for rape and fraud of the Swami Horos and her putative husband Theodore Horos – more prosaically Frank Jackson Dutton – founders of the Theocratic Unity Temple near Regent's Park. It was not the first time the Swami had been in court. But who was she? She claimed that she was born in Italy in 1854, the illegitimate daughter of King Ludwig I of Bavaria and the dancer Lola Montez and was sent to a cruel American foster family, the Salomons, in 1855.

If she was the daughter, it was an exceptionally long pregnancy because the last time Lola saw the King was in 1848. Sometimes she went by the names of Editha Lola Montez, Della Ann O'Sullivan or Solomon and more often as Diss Debar. She could also be found as Vera Ava, as well as Messant and McGoon, the surnames of men she seems to have married briefly.

Throughout her life she appeared regularly in the US courts. Working with her then husband 'General' Joseph Diss Debar and producing so-called 'spirit paintings' by Old Masters, she managed to ensnare the elderly lawyer Luther Marsh into making over his town house on Madison Avenue to her. During the trial she announced that her guiding spirits Cicero and the Council of Ten had advised her to return the deeds and this she did. It was wise advice and possibly reduced her sentence because on 19 June 1888 she received a mere six months. The phrase, 'There's nothing like an old fool' applied. Luther does not seem to have learned his lesson because he was again swindled by another spiritualist in the early 1900s.

After her release she collected a further two years' imprisonment in Geneva, Illinois, again for fraud under the name Vera P. Ava. On 7 May 1899 she was expelled from New Orleans for swindling and on the sixteenth of that month she was sentenced to 30 days for a similar offence.

It is difficult to know how many marriage ceremonies she actually went through. Apart from the Jackson marriage she lived with Debar for a number of years and had a daughter, Dodo, by him. At her trial at the Old Bailey she claimed she had actually been married to Debar despite his view that he had the encumbrance of an earlier wife.

She certainly married Jackson – later known as Jackson Dutton – in a ceremony in 1889 in Louisana, giving her title as Princess Editha Lolita and her parents as King Ludwig and Lola Montez. In the middle 1890s the Jacksons came to England via Cape Town, where she had met with some success as a clairvoyant, to set up a 'Purity League'. Now they called themselves Swami Laura Horos and Theodore Horos and earned their living telling fortunes and divining for lost property. In one way or another, a number of girls were recruited to the Temple.

Free love seems to have been very much the order of the day, with the girls sharing a bed with the Swami and Theo turning up in the middle of night to tell them they were his spiritual brides even though no formal ceremony had been undertaken. Curiously, the girls did not seem to mind the so-called rape as much as the fact that their property was being pawned by the Swami, for they wrote friendly, even loving, letters to her even – as the papers used to say – after the alleged incidents had taken place.

On 25 September 1901 the pair were arrested in Birkenhead where they had been lecturing and brought to London to face charges of obtaining property by false pretences to which, as the weeks went on, were added the charges of rape and buggery.

In a fiery trial they defended themselves and, still sticking to her story that her father was German and her mother Spanish, she – rather than he – produced a bombshell. Theo was a castrato and therefore incapable of rape. Doctors were called but they found that, although he was indeed minus one testicle, the other was small but perfectly formed and in working order.

Jackson received 15 years and she seven. Curiously, she appears to have been a good influence in the prison, calming some of the more recalcitrant inmates at Aylesbury, and was released early on licence. She was last heard of in Cincinatti in 1909, again under the name Vera Ava, after which she disappeared completely. In 1915 Jackson, now head of the Philadelphian Order of the Crystal Circle, was charged with bigamously marrying a 70-year-old woman in Buffalo and swindling her.

Diss Debar was, wrote the magician Harry Houdini admiringly, 'One of the most extraordinary fake mediums and mystery swindlers the world has ever known. Cagliostro, by comparison, seems to have been an amateur.'

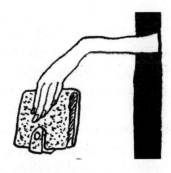

Out of this world

O N 23 APRIL 1726 Mary Toft, the wife of a clothier and mother of three children, claimed that while she had been weeding a field near Godalming, Surrey, she had been raped by a giant rabbit. The day was a significant part of her story, because St George's Day was then known as one on which magic forces were likely to be at work. Five months after the attack she complained of stomach pains and went to see John Howard, a surgeon in Guildford. A month after that Howard issued a statement that Toft had given birth to five baby rabbits. The birth was followed shortly after by the delivery of another seven.

This was perfectly believable. It was at a time when a physician had published a tract saying that a woman who stood too long and too near a hot stove during her pregnancy could give birth to rat-like creatures he named sooterkins. Now, Nathaniel St Andre, anatomist to the King and surgeon at Westminster Hospital, and Molyneux, the secretary to the Prince of Wales, visited her and both saw her deliver two more rabbits. A third surgeon was deceived, and she was only exposed when Sir Richard Manningham, the King's surgeon, sat up with her all night and ordered her to be kept under surveillance by doctors and nurses. There were no more births.

Discredited and arrested, she made a full confession. Her husband had supplied her with baby rabbits, which, while her observers were distracted, she had inserted *in vaginam* in time for delivery. She spent four months in the Bridewell before being released without a prosecution on 13 April 1827. Her story caused a temporary loss of income for rabbit catchers as well as a decline in the popularity of rabbit stew, but at least she can lay claim to be the mother of one of the most popular tricks in the magician's repertoire.

THE SO-CALLED last trial in England for witchcraft took place at the Old Bailey in March 1944. Although the prosecution was brought under the Witchcraft Act 1735 it was, in fact, simply a question of fraud. Usually, false mediums were tried under the Vagrancy Act and fined a few pounds, but Helen Duncan and three others, involved in a series of séances from the end of 1943 at the Master Temple Psychic Centre in Portsmouth, went before a jury.

Although her supporters denied it, claiming she had received a non-proven verdict, in 1934 Mrs Duncan had been fined £10 or one month in Edinburgh prison after she was exposed during a séance when the 'spirit' was found to be a woman's stockinette undervest. Two years earlier the psychic investigator Harry Price had denounced her as a fraud but this had done nothing to upset her popularity.

At the Portsmouth séance on 19 January 1944 she purportedly produced an ectoplasm which a police officer maintained was butter muslin. By the time of her arrest there was no trace of it and it was suggested that she was a regurgitator who could swallow things and bring them up again at will. Useful for a medium who is producing 'ectoplasm' from muslin.

She had upset the authorities who claimed she was making money out of the bereavement of families whose members had been killed on active service. Before it was officially announced at the end of January 1942, she had apparently materialised a sailor who said he had died when HMS *Barham* sank in November 1941. This information was being kept strictly secret by the government because the consequent loss of 841 lives would have been bad for the country's morale.

She served nine months' imprisonment and on her release she vowed never to take part in a séance again. However, in October 1956 the police raided a meeting in Nottingham where she was the medium. Her supporters claim that the ectoplasm produced burned her and, indeed, she went to hospital with second-degree burns. She died two months later on 6 December. Since her death there has been a continued, and so far unsuccessful, campaign to obtain a pardon for her.

Opinion is divided between those who believe she was the most gifted medium of her generation, an out and out fraud, or a medium who resorted to trickery only when her genuine powers began to fail.

THE YOUNG Fox sisters can be credited with the invention of modern spiritualism. In 1848 in upstate New York the 15-year-old Margaret, daughter of a Methodist clergyman, discovered she could crack her big toe so that it sounded like a knock on wood.

Her sister, Kate, called their parents and when she snapped her fingers three times what seemed to be a response of three knocks could be heard. The girls worked out a code and the spirits began to answer specific questions. From then on things escalated, and within months the girls were known nationwide, convincing millions that there was indeed an afterlife. The Fox girls were encouraged by their sinister, older, married sister Mrs Fish, and now appearances in Rochester produced $100 to $150 nightly. For a time Margaret gave up the life, but when her fiancé Dr John Kane died in 1857 she was left impoverished and returned to the circuit. For the next 30 years she and her sister carried out séances for up to $100 a client, profiting particularly during the American Civil War when grieving relatives wished to speak to those who had died.

Unfortunately they both became chronic alcoholics and, facing heavy criticism from scientists and clergymen and tiring of the game, Margaret, who had joined the Catholic Church, now decided to confess. On 21 October 1888 she gave an interview in which she stood shoeless on a table and cracked her toe. A headline in the *New York Herald* the next day read, HER BIG TOE DID IT ALL. Spiritualists would have none of it, saying she would have denounced her mother for $5, and that at the time of her confession she must have been drunk.

A<small>T THE END</small> of July 1917 16-year-old Elsie Wright and her ten-year-old cousin, Frances Griffiths, claimed that not only were they searching for fairies but they, indeed, had seen them at the bottom of the garden of Elsie's home in Cottingley, near Bradford. To prove it Elsie said she would take a photograph of them. Her father, Arthur, lent her a camera, and the results would cause debate and controversy for the next 70 years.

Arthur Wright developed the plates of their efforts and one of them showed Frances posing hand on chin, with a little waterfall in the background and four, winged fairies dancing on a bush nearer to the camera. One was playing what seemed to be a flute. The waterfall was blurred but the fairies were quite clear. Wright immediately believed his daughter had faked the picture with cardboard cut outs, but two months later Frances took a second picture. This time it showed Elsie sitting on the lawn talking to a gnome who was stepping on her skirt. Wright was still convinced the pair had faked the photographs but his wife Polly, who was interested in the mystical, thought they were genuine. Prints were passed to neighbours and friends and when Polly attended a meeting of the Bradford Theosophical Society in 1919 she showed the speaker the photographs. The next year Harold Snelling, a photographic expert, examined the prints and pronounced himself satisfied with them. From there they went to Sir Arthur Conan Doyle, a man who desperately wanted to believe in the spirit world. He, too, was convinced. Negatives were sent to Kodak who declined to certify their authenticity but were unable to explain how the fakes – if fakes they were – could have been done in so short a time and so cleverly by a young girl. One of the panel took the pragmatic view that since fairies couldn't be true they must be fakes.

Conan Doyle wanted to be convinced and arranged for the girls to be given a camera with marked plates. Suspicious, they insisted that the fairies would not appear if others, particularly disbelievers, were present. Left on their own, they produced two more plates, one with a fairy offering a flower to Elsie. The writer was delighted and in 1920 published his article on fairies with two photographs in the *Strand* magazine. It was a sensation. He also arranged for Geoffrey Hodson, a clairvoyant, to sit with the girls. Hodson reported that he had seen some wood elves as well as fairies when he was with the girls. In 1925 he published his conclusions that the girls and their photographs were completely genuine.

It was not until after both girls had died in the 1980s that the truth came out. Elsie had simply copied pictures from *Princess Mary's Gift Book*, cut them out and the pair had arranged them with hairpins. Afterwards they had rather callously drowned the cut-out fairies in the stream in the garden. In March 2001 the plates and negatives were sold for just under £6,000 at Bonhams, the London auction house.

THE SO-CALLED Cock Lane ghost nearly left Norfolk innkeeper William Kent facing a murder charge. He had something of an unhappy life. In early 1759 his wife Elizabeth died in childbirth and the child also died. He then fell in love with his wife's sister Fanny but by law could not marry her. They came to London and rented rooms in Cock Lane from the drunken Richard Parsons, then the officiating clerk of the church of St Sepulchre without Newgate.

While Kent was away at a wedding in November 1759 Parsons's daughter, also named Elizabeth, shared the bed with Fanny and that night there was the sound of scratching in the wainscotting. Over the days this developed into bangings, rapping and crashings. London became fascinated.

Meanwhile, Kent had lent his landlord 12 guineas, which he declined to repay. Solicitors were instructed and the Kents moved out. On 2 February 1760 Fanny died of smallpox and Kent married again. Back at Cock Lane the manifestations became louder and more frequent. Parsons had a carpenter in and when this failed to provide an explanation, he asked the assistant preacher at St Sepulchre, the Rev. John Moore, to intervene. A code was devised and the entity began to answer questions. Yes, Fanny had been poisoned by Kent with red arsenic and purl, a drink of warmed and spiced ale. Yes, Fanny hoped Kent would hang. In fact, the knockings, when she was alive, had been from her sister Elizabeth warning her.

In January 1762 Kent heard about the allegations and went to one of the séances now being held regularly at Cock Lane. When the accusations were again rapped out he stood up and denounced them. The following month, Dr Samuel Johnson was a member of a committee set up to investigate, which also denounced the apparent poltergeist as a sham. Then Parsons's daughter was caught hiding a sounding board in her bed. It was all over. Parsons was sentenced to two years and three trips to the pillory, his wife received a year and Moore, along with the editor of the *Public Ledger* who had printed the story, were ordered to pay Kent £588. There seems to be no record of

what happened to Elizabeth Parsons. For a time a Cock Lane Tale
became a synonym for a Cock and Bull story.

THE GREATEST of the nineteenth-century American spiritualist
fakers, Daniel Dunglas Home, known as 'King of the Spook World',
died on 21 June 1886 in Paris at the age of 53.

Born in 1833 in Scotland, he claimed his father was the natural son
of the tenth Earl of Home, and that his mother had second sight.
Taken to the US at the age of nine, he left home in Waterford,
Connecticut, at the age of 17 and within four years was the most
celebrated medium in the US. He then left to conquer Europe where,
for nearly 20 years, he held innumerable séances attended by such
royalty as Maximilian of Bavaria, the King and Queen of Württem-
berg, Alexander II of Russia and Napoleon III.

His most celebrated deceit was that of the Empress Napoleon,
whom he knew would wish to contact her dead father. When the
Empress touched a manifestation of his right hand she recognised it
immediately because the third finger was missing; Home had smuggled in a rubber replica. His most celebrated levitation was, so wit-
nesses said, his exit from a window on the third floor of a building
and his reappearance in another room. Another of his party pieces,
of a spirit concertina apparently playing 'Home Sweet Home' and
the 'Last Rose of Summer', both of which have a very limited range
of notes, may be explained by his collection of small mouth organs.

In October 1871 he married the Russian Julia de Gloumeline and
effectively retired. He was well advised to do so because now began
what might be called a witch-hunt of mediums. Although there was
one nasty incident in 1866 when a widow claimed she was conned
out of £60,000 – the action went against him and he returned the
money – in all the years he practised Home was one of the few
mediums of the time who was never exposed as a fraud. Never-

theless, all his apparent manifestations, the levitations and moving furniture, have been performed in magic and circus acts by a variety of magicians.

Even when efforts are made to expose fraudulent mediums they are not always well rewarded. In 1928 reporters from *Le Journal de Paris* obtained entrance to a séance at a house in Mantes sur Seine run by a Mme Alexandre and her gardener-husband, Blaise. The medium was Mme Alexandre and the spirit control, the voice through which the medium communicates with the dead, was Alexandre's daughter Madeleine who had died in 1918. It was illegal to charge fees for admission so Club Alexandre was formed to keep out the wary and uncommitted.

During the séance, when Madeleine was about to appear the gramophone started playing *Berceuse de Jocelyn*; Madeleine manifested herself, embraced her mother, played a few notes on the piano and distributed some flowers. The reporters noticed that Madeleine was wearing braces. One took hold of an arm and the other a collar and shone a torch on Blaise, now seen in his shirt sleeves with a mass of white cotton hiding his face. The reporters yelled, 'Fraud,' the Alexandres yelled, 'Spies, do not let them escape.' The reporters received a beating and were thrown out on to the street.

The next day, the reporters went to the local magistrate and pressed charges. At the hearing, the Alexandres told the court that the men were injured when they fell down the stairs trying to escape. Since he did not charge money there was no fraud on the part of Blaise. As for Madeleine, she had retired behind the curtain. Mme Alexandre produced a number of testimonials including one from the former President of Portugal. The charges against the Alexandres were dismissed and the reporters committed for trial.

In May 1999 a man claiming to be a Martian lost his lawsuit against The Royal College of Dental Surgeons in Canada and a number of other defendants whom he accused of a plot to conceal his Martian origins. The judge ruled that as Rene Joly was, on his own account, neither a human nor a corporation he had no standing in an Ontario court.

Dr Fritz, allegedly the ghost of a German doctor who died in the First World War, invades the bodies of Brazilians, turning them into healers. The first lucky recipient was Ze Arigo who apparently cured thousands of sick people who came from all over the country to be treated by him with an old pocketknife, a heavy German accent and absolutely no regard for medical hygiene. After surgery, the patients were given prescriptions written in Dr Fritz's illegible hand which could only be deciphered by Arigo's brother, who just happened to be a pharmacist. Two convictions for practising medicine illegally did nothing to dent Ze Arigo's reputation.

When Arigo died in a car crash in 1971 Dr Fritz moved on to inhabit the unlikely named Oscar Wilde for a short time, but he, too, died a violent death in another car crash. Dr Fritz next appeared in the guise of Edson Queiroz, a gynaecologist, who treated many patients as Dr Fritz before his life, too, was cut short when he was stabbed to death in 1991. The good doctor is currently working through the body of a well-educated Sao Paulo engineer whose healing power includes some psychic surgery with unconventional instruments such as scissors. Despite the engineer being accused of practising medicine without a licence, hundreds of patients line up, waiting all day long for treatment in the hope of a miraculous cure. The current incumbent has also predicted his own violent death within a few years.

In 1966 Nigerian-born Kayode Orishagbemi opened what he called the 'London Girls Modern College' in Finsbury Park, London, and wrote to rich Nigerians saying he would be willing to pay the fares of students to come to London. There was no such college. He also invited them to send him £1,000 so they could star in what he was projecting as an all-black version of *Cleopatra*.

It ended with disaster and with Orishagbemi being charged with the murder of 19-year-old machinist Grace Fayomi, found in Hampstead stuffed into a cardboard box. Fayomi had been living with Orishagbemi and his wife and the police said she had been killed to prevent her from telling all about the college. Orishagbemi maintained she was a practising witch and that:

> I just tied her up to the door. Very kindly I did it. She must have some kind of punishment so I beat her. After a long time she told me all about witchcraft and how she killed two other people. That is how she met her death. Witchcraft caused her death. I am responsible only for the parcel.

His statement went on to say that Grace worked witchcraft in her sleep, adding that she used a spider and would 'tie you up in the spider's web and you cannot move'. There was also a peanut which became invisible when someone was put in it and which could fly over rivers.

The trial judge ruled that belief in witchcraft was no defence to murder and Orishagbemi received life imprisonment. The judge had the police make further enquiries about the safety of any girl who might have come to London to attend the College.

IN 1985 ALICE Auma, of the Acholi tribe which was in conflict with Ugandan government forces, claimed to be possessed by the spirit of a dead Italian army officer named Lakwena. She went insane and, after the failure of 11 witches to cure her, help was provided by animals in the Paraa National Park where she spent a symbolic 40 days before returning as a spirit medium.

The next year, Lakwena ordered her to create a Holy Spirit Movement, the laudable short-term aims of which were to liberate the world from sin and bring an end to the civil war. The longer-term objectives were to bring about the Second Coming of Christ and introduce a paradise on earth.

After she managed to convince the leaders of the Ugandan People's Democratic Army to place troops under her control, she persuaded the soldiers that by smearing themselves with nut oil and taking magic potions they would be invulnerable to bullets. She also provided them with stones which, when blessed, were to explode like grenades. Sadly, it was not to be. In August 1987 her troops were mown down by machine-gun fire. Lakwena deserted her and she fled to Kenya where she remained in exile preaching to a dwindling flock until her death in January 2007.

In Britain, in the last few years, a scam has targeted black communities with conmen claiming to be spiritualists who can heal relationships and diseases. Often flyers are distributed through letterboxes or handed out on the streets. Sometimes, but more rarely, direct approaches are made. Victims are often required to pay a substantial amount for animal parts which are said to be necessary for the treatment or cure.

Horatio Bottomley

ORN IN BETHNAL Green in 1860, Horatio Bottomley was a larger-than-life character of enormous energy and intellect. He was also a talented speaker and writer and became a popular MP. He first worked for a solicitor who drank and a managing clerk who was as crooked as a corkscrew. The managing clerk was prosecuted but, before Bottomley left the law to become a court shorthand writer, he learned his trade well.

From then on, he appeared in over 40 major trials, always as a litigant or defendant in person. Bottomley was first arrested for fraud in 1893 when, perhaps, he was fortunate with his judge, Mr Justice Hawkins, who was partial to rogues. He was also fortunate that the prosecution case was weak. It is said that after Bottomley's acquittal, Hawkins suggested he take up law and that on qualification he would give him his own wig. Instead Bottomley became MP for South Hackney in 1906 under the Liberal banner and was re-elected in 1910, but his field was really creative finance and a brilliant understanding of cross-examination. However, in 1912 he went bankrupt to the tune of the enormous sum of £233,000 and lost his seat. In 1914 he was convicted at Bow Street on a charge of running an illegal lottery but the Court of Appeal quashed the conviction. Then in 1918 he was back in politics, successful as an Independent. In the meantime he bought and founded such papers and magazines as *John Bull*, devoted to exposing roguery, and promoted such grandly titled fraudulent companies as the Joint Stock Trust and Finance Corporation.

As a sideline there were quality racehorses that won classics, a manor house and an ever increasing amount of champagne. Hugely sentimental, he never sold one of his horses if he could help it.

It is thought that his swindles netted him around £50 million at today's rates. The last of these was the Victory Bond Swindle, which earned him £80,000. Working on the principle of the wholly admirable Premium Bonds, it was basically a lottery with investors able to draw their capital. Unfortunately, in short order, the whole of the money disappeared into Bottomley's pockets and those of his creditors. He received seven years, served five and re-launched himself as a lecturer. He collapsed and died in 1933 while appearing at the Windmill theatre in London in a one-man show.

The most-told story of him is that when Prime Minister Andrew Bonar Law visited Wormwood Scrubs, there was Bottomley working the stitching machine. 'Sewing, Bottomley?' asked Bonar Law. 'No, sir, reaping.' But the same story is told about Oscar Wilde. During his sentence, Bottomley made regular visits to the Bankruptcy Court in his own clothes. When it was pointed out to him that his coat was rather creased he replied, 'When I get back I change for dinner.'

There's a sucker born every minute

WILLIAM MILLER, born in 1874, is the man credited with devising the modern 'robbing Peter to pay Paul' scheme. First he developed a credit rating by repaying his debts and then set himself up as an investment adviser in Brooklyn, New York. He was also helped by the fact that he taught a Bible class and persuaded his flock that he could obtain 10 per cent interest on their investments. When they replied incredulously that this was four times what banks paid he announced that it was 10 per cent per week or 520 per cent per annum.

He set up the Franklin Syndicate, trading on the name of the former President, and the first investors were repaid their interest promptly. Now money poured in to an extent that he was making around $430,000 a month. There were hiccups, however, and the first was that he was obliged to pay protection money to an Edward Schlesinger. Then, when it was clear the scheme was running out of steam, he gave what he said was his entire remaining capital of $240,000 to a lawyer, Robert Ammon, on the understanding that Ammon would send him regular payments; he then fled to Canada. The lawyer never did and Miller was retrieved in February 1900 and in June sentenced to ten years. The term was reduced when in 1907 he gave evidence against Ammon who was also charged with fraud. Miller disappeared shortly afterwards with, it was suspected, money he had held back from Ammon.

CHARLES PONZI, who emigrated to the US from Italy at the end of the nineteenth century, discovered he could buy international postal reply coupons in some countries at below face value. They could then be resold in the US at a profit of up to 50 per cent. His first venture netted him $1,250.

Now, based on this scheme, he offered investors 50 per cent on their money, payable in three months, which was later cut to 45 days. Once he started paying the interest more money poured into his offices. He bought land and a brokerage company and, for himself, 200 suits, 24 diamond stick pins, 48 gold-handled Malacca canes and a life-style to go with them. Then in 1920 the *Boston Post* printed an article that Ponzi had served time for cheque frauds in Canada and for smuggling immigrants. The rot set in, particularly when it was shown there were not enough international reply coupons in the whole world to back his scheme. The default was reckoned to be somewhere between $5 million and $10 million, but it could have been more.

He was sentenced to five years and then a further conviction followed in Massachusetts. He absconded to Florida while on bail and began a land swindle. It was then on to Texas before he was sent back to Massachusetts. After he had served that seven-to-nine-year sentence he was deported to Italy where he is thought to have swindled the government. He made his way to Brazil where he worked for an airline, ran a hot-dog stall and, before his death in a charity ward in Rio de Janeiro in January 1949, taught English and French for a living.

FROM THEN ON the scam became known as the Ponzi Swindle. One in Portugal, paying a relatively modest 10 per cent, was run by Maria Branca dos Santos for nearly 14 years from 1970. She received ten years in 1988. In September 2003, Reed Eliot Slatkin, an ordained minister of the Church of Scientology, was sentenced to 14 years following a Ponzi Swindle which had taken upwards of $200 million, said to be the largest since the ones run by the great man himself. Some of the funds had been sent to various churches. The Church of Scientology agreed to refund $3.5 million.

With the coming of the Millennium, the public was ripe for a scam to persuade them that champagne would be at a premium on the great evening. In 1996 and 1997 three men began a promotion selling champagne, promising to hold the £30 bottles until they were auctioned in London shortly before the end of the century when huge profits could be expected. No auctions took place, the champagne could be bought for £12 and it was of a lesser quality than cheaper brands. The three principals in the scheme, which targeted professionals and retirees, went to prison. Two of them had operated a similar whisky fraud out of Gibraltar during the early 1990s. Even if things had been on the level there was never going to be a shortage. The champagne houses had already increased growth to cope with potential demand.

Another Millennium scam was the telephone fraud from the US. The conmen purported to be calling from the victim's bank saying there was a problem with the Millennium bug. Money could be switched to an account which was fully Y2K compliant but details of the old account were needed.

WHEN THE BSE crisis of 1995 turned consumers away from beef, ostrich meat was put forward as the new alternative. Martin Evans, an undischarged bankrupt, set up the Ostrich Breeding Company near Swansea, taking over £850,000 from investors who were promised returns of up to £85,000 on an adult breeding bird at a cost of £12,900. Within a year the company was in liquidation and around £400,000 had been siphoned off by Evans into overseas accounts. He disappeared and resurfaced as an international drug smuggler. He was not arrested until 2001 when he received 21 years. In December 2006 he was ordered to pay £4.8 million or serve a further eight years on top of the 21 he was doing. For once it seems the investors may get their money back.

ABROAD, THE penalties for being discovered may be more severe. In February 2007 Wang Zhendong, the chairman of a Chinese trading company in Liaoning province, was sentenced to death after swindling over 10,000 investors out of £200 million in a scam to breed ants to be used in making tea, wine and medicine, the last of which would be used to cure arthritis. Packets of ants worth £13 were sold for up to £660 with assurances of returns from 35 to 60 per cent.

He was not the first swindler to be sentenced to death in China in recent months. In December 2006 the High Court upheld the sentence of an accountant who had defrauded bank customers by offering fake accounts at high interest rates.

In the late summer of 1926 H. Joshua Phillips sought a partner willing to invest £500 in his invention, the Torgoscope, a machine for the production 'of internal iridescence and opalescence in transparent and translucent bodies', or, how to manufacture precious stones and gems from worthless materials. £200 was to be paid up front and the balance at £10 per week for a half share in either the proceeds or a machine outright. Part of the machine would be manufactured by outside engineers who would have no idea of the 'wonderful nature of the mechanism they were handling'. Phillips would put the finishing touches to the invention.

On questioning, Phillips admitted he had not yet succeeded in making any opals, diamonds or pearls. He had nevertheless a lady of title in the wings waiting to invest, as well as a millionaire friend just about to do so. The applicant withdrew.

Artur Virgilio Alves dos Reis began life in humble circumstances – he was the son of an undertaker – but he worked his way to the very top and down again. Born in Lisbon in 1898, at the age of 18 he emigrated to the Portuguese colony of Angola. He forged himself a diploma of engineering and obtained a job as a supervising engineer for a railroad. With an uncleared cheque he bought himself a major stake in the Trans African Railways of Angola and he was up and running. He returned to Lisbon where he forged cheques to finance the purchase of an ailing company, Ambaca, using its finances to cover the cheques and to buy shares in the Angola Mining Company. He was arrested but released on a technicality.

Now he embarked on his major scheme and the one for which he is remembered. He forged a contract in the name of the Bank of Portugal, which deceived the English security printers, Waterlows, into believing that he and his associates were permitted to print banknotes for Portugal. These had the same numbers as those of real notes but should have been stamped 'Angola' and used only in that country. Reis then laundered the notes into smaller denominations of genuine money, and used the enormous profits to create the Bank of Angola and Metrópole. His ultimate aim was to buy a controlling interest in the Bank of Portugal, which would make it unlikely that he would ever be investigated, but a teller in Oporto became suspicious, enquiries began and banknotes with duplicated serial numbers were found.

Reis was arrested in 1925 and five years later sentenced to 20 years. His forged documents were so convincing that for a while Bank of Portugal officials were suspected of being involved. Reis was released in May 1945 and later convicted of a coffee fraud. He died in poverty in 1955. His fraud had enormous long-term consequences for Portugal's economy and politics. The currency was severely compromised by the counterfeiting and there was a crisis of confidence in the Portuguese government which, in turn, led to the dictatorship of Antonio de Oliveira Salazar.

THE BOILER Room originated in the 1920s when telephone salesmen huddled round a stove to make their pitches selling worthless stock. There are many advantages in using the telephone, not least that the victim is never in a position to identify the salesman nor is there any need for elaborate equipment as there is with a Big Store operation. In the 1950s and 1960s one of the most lucrative of these in the US was selling swamp land in Florida. Boiler Rooms are often located in South California and Florida because of the accessibility of drugs. 'It's also a lot more fun to have $500,000 in Beverly Hills than it is in Bismark,' said one worker.

Today a Boiler Room operation is highly complex. The victim cold-called on the telephone may hear a convincing background babble which may be genuine or may be taped. Sometimes Boiler Room frauds will start with newsletters which are followed up with a call. In a process known as 'pump and dump' the caller will then push a small stock, possibly one even quoted on, say, the Nasdaq, which the promoters hold almost entirely. Share certificates are often not sent out. If the victim tries to call the broker, there is only a message on an answering machine.

IN THE EARLY 1980s, the Fort Lauderdale-based International Gold Bullion Exchange run by the Alderdice brothers, William and James, took over $100 million from 13,000 investors across the country. They were supposedly purchasing gold and then storing it in their vaults. It may have begun as a legitimate business but by the time it failed there were 100 telephone representatives working from the company's Boiler Rooms.

Between 1980 and 1982 the company grossed $130 million but, when the scam collapsed the following year and the authorities broke into the vault, all they found were five pieces of wood painted gold, an adding machine and a copy of *Playboy*. Investors lost everything. The brothers owned a mine in Alaska which they said would repay the investors, but since it was under water nothing came of it.

There were other troubles as well for the brothers. While they were in prison trying to raise money for their bail they had met James Doyle who came to live with them as bodyguard, chauffeur and partner in a chicken-raising business. The idea was that if the lights were turned on and off the chickens would be fooled into thinking it was another day and so lay more eggs. On 15 July 1984 Doyle stabbed William Alderdice to death and cut James badly. The motive was never clearly established, but there were suggestions that it was a contract killing on behalf of the Mob who had lost money in the Exchange. Doyle maintained he had broken up a fight between the brothers and then, when he went into William's room to get his bathing costume, William had gone berserk.

Charged with 203 theft and fraud charges in Illinois, New York and Florida, in a plea-bargain James Alderdice was sentenced to two concurrent terms of five years. In prison in Tallahassee he studied the Bible, and on his release became youth minister for the First Assembly of God in Glendale, Arizona.

BOTH LONDON and Paris were entertained during the first six months of 1908 with the swindle by Henri Lemoine of rue Pigalle, Montmartre, on Julius Wernher of the De Beers Diamond Mine company. Over the previous three years Wernher had paid a total of £64,000 after the Frenchman had apparently discovered a process to produce gem-sized diamonds from coal and had agreed to sell his secret to Wernher.

The magnate had gone to Lemoine's workshop where the man had stripped naked and mixed substances in a crucible, and 15 minutes later produced 20 well-formed diamonds. Asked to repeat the experiment he did so.

The secret formula was then sealed and lodged in a London bank and all went well until the experiment was repeated in the presence of an engineer from De Beers who was not satisfied. Wernher then brought criminal proceedings which were hotly contested in Paris by Lemoine. Now jewellers came forward to say they recognised stones sold by them to Mme Lemoine.

In his defence, Lemoine offered to reproduce his experiment in front of the magistrate and counsel. He was allowed bail to do so but failed on the first occasion, claiming that the German-made crucible was not up to standard. Invited to try once more on 17 June 1908 and told that if he failed he would be sent for trial, Lemoine disappeared.

There had been considerable trouble getting the bank to produce the envelope with the secret formula, but after proceedings in the High Court in London it was sent over to Paris and opened. To everybody's fury it contained a formula that could have been devised by a schoolboy and which could be reduced to, 'Take carbon, crystallise it, and submit it to sufficient pressure. You will have diamonds.'

It seems that Lemoine had intended to raise funds and then produce the secret formula which would, he believed, have caused a run on De Beers shares. He would then have bought in and made a killing on the market. He was not retrieved until April 1909 and two months later received six years.

LITTLE CHANGES. During the First World War, Louis Enricht invented a cheap substitute for petrol. All that was needed was for water to be added. In 1916 he duly gave a press conference in Farmingdale, Long Island. One of the reporters was told to bring a bucket of water into which Enricht poured a green substance and then filled the petrol tank of his car. Off it went, smelling of almonds.

Enricht admitted that cyanide was a constituent of the invention but until he obtained a patent he would not disclose anything further. Investment funds poured in, including money from the financier Hiram Maxim who put in $100,000. Another banker put in a similar amount and in return received a sealed envelope purporting to contain the formula, but not to be opened before the patent was granted. When there was a rumour that Enricht was a German spy, the banker opened the envelope to find only two Liberty Bonds. Enricht escaped prosecution on this occasion.

Then in 1920 Enricht announced he had another invention for turning peat into petrol and, once more, in poured the money. This time, however, the Nassau County district attorney investigated and found that the investors' money had gone on gambling. Invited in court to show that he could produce petrol from peat Enricht failed and, in November 1922, received seven years for grand larceny. He was paroled on the grounds of ill health and died the next year.

The trick was worked with a mixture of acetone and liquid acetylene. It would run a car for a time but would ultimately ruin the engine. The cyanide masked the smell of the acetone. Even without ruining the engine it would have been more expensive than petrol.

EXACTLY THE same scam was worked by Guido Franch, from Livingston, Illinois, for nearly three decades from the 1950s. He took money from a number of small investors and claimed that the oil industry would have his invention suppressed if he disclosed the formula of his water-into-gasoline powder.

Even more recently, the con was worked in India by high-school dropout Ramar Pillai who claimed he could produce diesel fuel by boiling leaves from a special plant in water for 30 minutes. For a while, he managed to hoodwink the scientific community and the public until the Indian Institute of Technology called his bluff; in March 2000 he admitted the substance was not herbal fuel. It is thought he may have been part of a gang who hoped to trick people into buying fuel they had stolen from oil companies.

Frank Abagnale

IN THE 1960s, the multi-talented and disciplined Frank Abagnale began his career as a conman creating a series of identities to go with his multiple bank accounts opened to keep his cheques from bouncing. In the days when banks permitted drawing against uncleared cheques he began printing his own, cashing them and obtaining money before they bounced.

Later, he posed as Frank Williams, a Pan-Am airline pilot, to get free trips on scheduled airline flights, a process known as 'deadheading'. From then it was a short step to making a counterfeit Pan-Am ID card and an FAA pilot's licence. He obtained a uniform by pretending he had lost his.

Then came a spell as a doctor in Georgia where he became a resident supervisor, a position he held for 11 months. By this time he had forged a Harvard University Law degree and after passing, possibly legitimately, the Louisiana bar examination, he worked for the state attorney's office, resigning when a man with a genuine Harvard degree joined the staff.

After forging another degree, this time from Columbia University, it was time to go teaching sociology at Brigham Young University in Utah. He then became engaged and when his fiancée rather unsportingly told the police of his exploits he went on the run.

He stayed out for five years, cashing bad cheques for over $2.6 million in 26 countries before he was arrested. In France he served a short sentence, nearly dying of pneumonia before he was extradited to Sweden. Deported to the US he was sentenced to 12 years in a Federal prison.

He was released in 1974 and for a short time worked for the US government advising on anti-fraud schemes. He then wrote to a bank offering to give a lecture on fraud for $50 – no satisfaction, no fee. They were well satisfied and he went on to establish a consultancy, advising against fraud. Now a multi-millionaire, his autobiography *Catch Me If You Can* was filmed with Leonardo DiCaprio.

The Spanish Prisoner strikes again, and again, and again ...

IN THE MIDDLE OF November 1905 Paul Webb, a shopkeeper of Lower Sloane Street, received a letter from Barcelona. By just after Christmas he had received four more and he took them to Scotland Yard. The first one had been sent by Louis Ramot, then a prisoner in the military fortress in Barcelona. It asked for the relatively modest sum of £59. If it was sent, Webb would receive a share of £37,000, which was already lodged in a British bank.

Webb had been selected as a potential victim of the Spanish Prisoner Swindle which, in one form or another, has run since the Armada. The letter dated 11 November 1905 began:

Although I only have the honour of being acquainted with you by the reference that my dear wife, a relative of yours gave me and that remembering the personalities of our family always wondered the honesty and good qualities that distinguished you, I address myself to you perhaps for the first and last time because the graveness of my health compels me to may [sic] you know of my sad position and beg your assistance and protection for my only daughter, Mary, a young girl fourteen years old who is now in a Pension House, owing inform you that my deceased wife was Mrs Elizabeth Webb.

He went on to ask for complete discretion as he was being watched by his enemies and to say that he had been the private secretary and treasurer of General Martinez Campos in the last Cuban war and, as a result, had been able to provide for his motherless daughter. He had deserted, decamping with £37,000. He had intended to go with his daughter to the US, and set sail for Spain to collect her. There he was

recognised, arrested for desertion and sentenced to 16 years' penal servitude.

His luggage, which contained a secret drawer with the details of the bank account, had been impounded and the £59 was required for its release. The letter was being sent with the help of his best friend, the prison chaplain. Poor Ramos did not expect to survive much longer and if Mr Webb would undertake the care and guardianship of his daughter then he could have a quarter of the £37,000. If Webb could help he was to send a telegram 'Send Samples – Webb' to Richard, Lista de Correos, Vich, Barcelona. Webb replied, and received a letter within days:

> Very agreeable has been to me just in these sad and trying moments your cablegram; thanks to your kindness and good heart I shall die satisfied relying on the future of my daughter who shall have a strong and kind protector.

Jean Richard was the prison chaplain and after these two letters he took over the correspondence, sending a clipping to show the death of poor Luis Ramos who had succumbed to hepatitis, 'after approaching God and receiving the last Holy Sacrament'. He also sent along the death certificate from the prison sealed by the Governor and the Administrator.

Similar letters were sent around the same time to a Mr S. Topey of Woolwich and a Mr Thomas McGill. On 6 March 1907 Mary Bates, a newsagent of Compton Street, received a letter addressed to her husband. This time the prisoner had been sentenced in France for wounding a policeman and had 32,000 livres of which she could have a quarter. Since her husband had been dead for seven years and she knew no one in France anyway, she took the letter to the police.

Now efforts were made to try to establish just how widespread was the trick, and other victims were found in Dublin, Manchester, Cherbourg and Welshpool. A Mrs Margaret McAllister in Clackmananshire had agreed to act as the orphan girl's guardian. She sent £60. The good Father, flushed with his success, asked for a further £45 for legal expenses.

The swindle continued until 1908 when it temporarily died away. It was revived during the First World War, this time with the story of a Belgian who, on the death of his master at the siege of Liège, had fled to Spain with £20,000 Bank of England notes. The authorities inserted a notice in a number of newspapers to the effect that it was a scam, and again the swindle seems to have died down.

It has, however, resurfaced throughout the world in various guises. It was popular in Germany in the 1930s when many people were genuinely trying to get their money out of Nazi clutches. More recently, British soldiers have discovered a cache of Al-Qaeda gold in Afghanistan and need help in getting it out of the country. Other new examples have been: the war correspondent who has found Saddam Hussein's missing millions, victims of Hurricane Katrina, the London 7 July 2005 bombings and a young orphan from the tsunami of 26 December 2004 wanting help to move her parents' millions out of an overseas bank.

THE SWINDLE has also long been popular in the US where the prisoners are in Mexico. Apparently doctors are prime victims in the scam in which, for added spice, the punter goes south of the Rio Grande and is then told he is a wanted man. Only with the help of corrupt police or prison guards can he escape imprisonment, and his money is removed at various stages before he struggles back to the border clutching that important and worthless number of a safe deposit box in a bank somewhere in Texas. In a fit of generosity the US courts have ruled that there can be tax relief for those duped by this swindle.

NIGERIAN fraudsters have turned the Spanish Prisoner letter into an art form known as 419, after the applicable section of the Nigerian Penal Code. Government money has gone missing and the writer knows where it is. You can share in this; you do not need to send money just the details of your bank account.

The Nigerian fraudsters are now also working a variation on a personal basis. If you have dealt with someone in the country then you may get a call to say he is in hospital awaiting an emergency operation which must be financed privately. If you ring back you even get to speak to the 'surgeon'.

IT IS NOT ONLY the dupe's bank account which is in danger from Nigerian fraudsters. In 2001 a former deputy Mayor of Northampton found himself in a serious situation after he received one of the 25,000 odd letters sent to Britain annually inviting him to supply his bank details so that fraudsters, who maintained they were working for the Nigerian Civil Service, could transfer a large sum of money. The man would, in return, receive a substantial commission. On 8 July, he flew to Johannesburg to meet his future business partners. He was promptly kidnapped and taken to a house on East Rand where £20,000 was demanded for his release. A joint operation between the Northampton police, the National Crime Squad and the South African police ended when three men were arrested as they went to the bank to collect the ransom.

TODAY, IN A scam known as the Advance Fee Fraud, victims are contacted to say they have won a substantial prize in a foreign lottery or inherited a substantial amount. They must then send money to pay the necessary tax due and administrative expenses. This may be a relatively small amount compared with the winnings or inheritance. In recent years the 'Canadian National Lottery' has been popular; Canada has no national lottery. Another scam uses the name of the real El Gordo lottery in Spain. So if you receive an email or a letter claiming you have won in the El Gordo Lottery – or any number of other lotteries – and you have not bought a ticket, you have been selected for another modern-day version of the Spanish Prisoner scam. You will be required either to pay an advance fee to access the prize or to give details of your bank account so the 'prize' can be sent direct. This provides the scammers with enough information for identity theft or to access your account.

VERY SIMILAR IS the advertisement which offers fast loans irrespective of the applicant's credit history. Some are genuine but others require fees up front to pay for administration and insurance. Once the fee is paid the applicant hears no more. The same applies to offers of working from home. The victim is often required to put down a deposit as an act of good faith or for equipment at a highly inflated price.

EVEN THE apparently money-sophisticated can be duped. In 2002 a man falsely calling himself Sir Robert Scott Macmillan took $2 million from a German businessman after promising that, using emerging markets, he could double the man's investment within 20 to 30 days. The man never met Macmillan. All communication was through telephone, fax and emails.

PYRAMID SCHEMES and chain letters are very similar and very seductive as, in theory, they may deliver profits to a very few early investors. Chain letters, which are illegal in Britain, invite the recipient of the letter to send money to the person named at the top of a list, delete that name, add their own to the bottom and in turn send copies of the letter to a stated number of new people, who will all repeat the process. Even if everyone complies, it is impossible for the chain to continue for very long. It cannot expand beyond the size of the earth's population and with the usual send-this-message-to-five-people scheme, it takes less than 15 steps before the total number of participants must be 7.6 billion, well above the number of people in the world.

IN OCTOBER 1997 John G. Bennett Jnr, head of New Era Philanthropy, was sentenced to 12 years for carrying out what was described as the biggest charity fraud in US history. He defrauded donors and charities of $135 million by means of a classic pyramid scheme, promising to double the amount of a donor's gift in six months with funds from anonymous wealthy benefactors. Pyramid schemes demand an ever-accelerating cash flow and, like Miller, Ponzi and all the others, Bennett was using later donations to pay off outstanding double-your-money pledges while, at the same time, siphoning off at least $5 million for personal use and $3 million for use in his for-profit companies. Some 1,100 individuals and charities, including more than 180 evangelical groups, colleges and seminaries, lost an estimated $100 million. Bennett maintained he was driven not by criminal intent but by unrestrained religious fervour, a defence strategy the judge did not accept.

EMAIL PHISHING is another example of a scam to obtain sensitive information. These emails appear to come from a trustworthy source, such as your bank or credit card company, which has encountered a problem. The email asks for details of your account and password, and when you give this information away, you are financing the work of a criminal. Another version purports to come from HM Revenue & Customs saying you are eligible for a tax refund and requiring you to complete a form giving your bank details. The first recorded use of the word was probably in January 1996, but since then phishing has developed into a major fraud.

IN 2006 ENGLISHMAN Mike Berry, tired of attempts by conmen to take his money over the Internet, retaliated by asking the men to verify their identities by having themselves photographed holding a code word and then emailing the result to him. The codewords included 'Plonker', and variations included the emailer holding a fish in one hand and balancing a loaf of bread on his head. Another was required to write out a Harry Potter novel by hand to prove he was genuine.

IN 2001 THE 32-year-old restaurant busboy Abraham Abdallah from Brooklyn, New York, went to prison after being accused of stealing the identities of over 200 American celebrities including Stephen Spielberg, Martha Stewart and Oprah Winfrey.

Using the Internet and a copy of *Forbes* magazine which listed the 400 richest people in the US, Abdallah put together the home addresses, dates of birth and Social Security numbers of tycoons and chief executives and used them to trick credit companies to provide detailed reports. These were then used to persuade banks and brokers to transfer money into accounts controlled by him. He included telephone numbers where he could be reached and these were answered through voicemail in the victim's name. When arrested he was found to have over 800 fraudulent credit cards and some 20,000 blank ones. He claimed that his efforts had not been financially motivated but rather from an overpowering compulsion to beat the system.

THE LATEST version of phishing combined with other scams seems to be an email inviting the mark to open an account apparently with the Alliance and Leicester (although there will no doubt be other variations). A deposit of £500 on the fake website – complete with spelling errors and typos – will be rewarded with an immediate cheque for £200. Oh yes?

Melanie Mills

WOULD-BE AUTHORS have always been prey to unscrupulous literary agents who charge them large fees not to read their manuscripts. One who took things to exceptional lengths was Roswitha Von Meerscheidt-Hullessem, better known in the southern states of the US as Melanie Mills. In 2002 she was charging authors between $500 and $1,500 for editing services after wrongly telling them publishers had expressed interest in their work.

The next year, she organised a writers' conference in Myrtle Bay. It was cancelled at short notice and although punters, who had paid around $400 a head, were told it would be rescheduled, no date was ever announced. This may have been because, sadly, Ms Mills was killed in a car accident while visiting her family in Germany in the June.

At the time of her 'death', announced by Mills herself acting as her assistant, she was running frauds on the Internet as well as a vacation-rental scam. She reappeared in Banff, Alberta, as Elisabeth von Hullessem, organising a literary conference scheduled for that August at a charge of just under $1,700 a head, which did, at least, include accommodation. It had to be postponed, apparently because of forest fires in the region. Before the rescheduled date, Mills and the money had disappeared again. At the end of October, she was arrested in British Columbia.

She was, in fact, genuinely the daughter of a German Countess and in 1999 had lived in a trailer on her mother's land in Arkansas. That summer she announced that her mother had been killed in a car crash in Germany, and she filed the necessary papers to obtain $250,000 from the estate. Happily, like those of Mark Twain, the reports of her mother's death were premature. Unaware of her own demise, the Countess and her boyfriend returned at the end of their holiday and asked her daughter for a lift from the airport. An altercation between mother and daughter resulted in the Countess being pinned between a cement picnic table and the car. Charges, including battery and aggravated assault against her daughter, were followed by bail, and Ms Mills fled to Missouri and then to South Carolina where she set up her literary agency.

All in all Ms Mills, and her 15 aliases, came out of things very well. She got away almost with time served – the period she had spent awaiting her trial – in the Banff case and was extradited to Arkansas where she picked up 15 years, but all but twenty-three months were suspended. She was then deported to Canada where, it is said, she is trying to have her own memoirs published.

Fooling around

THE **SPAGHETTI FARM** remains one of the UK's most famous April Fool's Day jokes. In 1957 the respected *Panorama* programme, introduced by the distinguished broadcaster Richard Dimbleby and watched by an audience of eight million, featured a family in Switzerland carrying out their annual spaghetti harvest, plucking strands from a tree and laying them out in the sun to dry. Fresh pasta was virtually unknown in the UK in the 1950s and huge numbers were taken in by the hoax. The BBC reportedly told the many callers wanting to grow their own to 'place a sprig of spaghetti in a tin of tomato sauce and hope for the best'.

ON 1 APRIL 1977 the *Guardian* published a seven-page supplement commemorating the tenth anniversary of the independence of the small island of San Serriffe in the Indian Ocean. Its two islands were named Upper Caisse and Lower Caisse, its capital was Bodoni and its leader was General Pica. The many readers who sought more information about this idyllic holiday destination failed to notice the proliferation of printing terms with which all the people and places were named. Genuine advertisements appeared in the supplement and, joining in the fun, one advertiser offered a contest with the prize of a two-week trip to Cocobanana Beach on the island. San Serriffe became a running gag in the newspaper, reappearing on April Fool's Day in 1978, 1980 and 1999, each time moving to a different ocean.

In 1998 BURGER King issued a press release and took a full-page advertisement in *USA Today* announcing the introduction of a Left-Handed Whopper, which had the usual ingredients but with all the condiments rotated 180 degrees for the comfort of left-handed customers. Thousands flocked to the restaurants to order the new item and others requested their own right-handed version. Sales increased substantially for both versions.

In 1998 GUINNESS announced that it had reached an agreement with the Old Royal Observatory: throughout 1999 Greenwich Mean Time would be known as Guinness Mean Time in the run-up to the Millennium. In addition, where the Observatory traditionally counted seconds in 'pips', it would now count them in 'pint drips'. Having rather sniffily reported on the plan, the *Financial Times* was obliged to issue a curt retraction when it realised the whole thing had been an April Fool's joke.

As IF BEING sold twice was not sufficient, the Eiffel Tower suffered a further indignity when it was reported in 1986 by *Le Parisien* as its April Fool's joke that it was being moved to the new Euro Disney, east of Paris. It was to be replaced by a 35,000-seater stadium for the 1992 Olympics.

In 1953 Edward Watters of Austell, Georgia, bet a friend he could get his photograph in the newspapers within a fortnight. He bought a monkey for $50, killed it and, after shaving it from head to paw, cut off its tail. He then faked an accident on Highway 78, placing the

monkey in front of a truck. He was found by a patrolman wandering in the road talking of Martians and what seemed to be a spacecraft landing and disgorging these little things, one of which he had run over. He duly had his picture in the papers and won his $10 bet. The FBI and the US Air Force who were called in were not amused.

NEARLY 150 years earlier, Theodore Hook wagered his friend Sam Beazley that he would make 54 Berners Street, owned by the widow Tottingham, the most famous house in London. He wrote hundreds of letters and, as a result, on a given morning a dozen chimney sweeps arrived, followed by a wagon load of coal, then furniture, a hearse, midwives, two doctors and a dentist. As the morning went on so more and more tradesmen arrived and, it was said, so did the Lord Mayor of London and the Duke of York who had been told one of his officers was dying there. It was only when night came that order was restored. Hook went abroad until the fuss died down.

THE APRIL FOOL's joke by *The Times* in 1972 did not cause quite as much chaos. That year was the centenary of the first round-the-world tour by Thomas Cook Travel. *The Times* ran a full article on the tour and also noted that the first 1,000 applicants would be able to recreate the tour at the cost of the original, namely 210 guineas. Applications should be addressed to Miss Avril Foley. Huge queues formed outside the company's offices and those who had waited hours were by no means pleased.

Ten tips to beat the conman

1. **The Golden Rule** If you are offered anything which seems too good to be true, it almost certainly is. Remember that over £1 billion annually is lost to scams in the UK.

2. **Ask yourself 'Why Me?'** Why should I be so lucky to be receiving 25 per cent interest when building societies are only offering 5 per cent? Why if the returns are so good and the product is so safe should I be approached rather than major investment banks? Why is this nubile blonde I have met on the Internet taking such an interest in a middle-aged bald man, but does not have the fare to travel to London/Glasgow/Cardiff to meet me?

3. **Take your time** Do your own research into any proposed deal. Don't rush into things – speed and secrecy are the tools of the conman.

4. **Worry if you see the word FREE** It almost certainly won't be.

5. **Beware of handing over money** even if it appears that it will be put into an account to which the conman apparently has no access. Among the welter of paperwork there is likely to be some fine print which says that there is an order or power of attorney, which negates the main text of the document.

6. **If you have any doubts about a caller** – hang up.

7. **Don't respond to telephone calls** that say you have won a prize in a lottery you did not know you had entered. They are generally scams which require you to pay money for tax or expenses. You will receive no prize but will be charged for a call to a premium number.

8. **Don't return calls to taped messages** from an unknown source left on your answering machine or telephone. They will also

often be to premium numbers and you will either have to listen to a long recorded message or you will be kept talking for as long as possible while the conman benefits from every second you are on the line.

9. **Don't join a pyramid or chain letter scheme** – remember that with a chain letter sent on to only five people by each recipient, it takes less than 15 steps to exceed the world's population. Only those who set up the scheme make money from it.

10. **Don't take a cheque** – particularly from abroad, for more than the value of goods sold or services offered – for example, rent – and then refund the difference. The fact that the cheque has apparently been cleared by your bank will not save you when it is eventually dishonoured, as it almost certainly will be.

Select Bibliography

Michael Gilbert includes Horatio Bottomley and John Stonehouse in his *Fraudsters*. Gene Fowler's *The Great Mouthpiece* is a roaring account of the life and crimes of the New York lawyer Bill Fallon.

Victor Lustig wrote his self-serving memoirs *The Man who sold the Eiffel Tower*. The adventures of Sophie Lyons and Annie Gleason as well as Princess Soltikoff are included in James Morton, *Gangland: The Early Years*. Sophie Lyons also wrote *Crime Does Not Pay!*, intended to show that is exactly what it does.

There are a number of books about Mary Baker, Princess Caraboo, including John Wells, *Princess Caraboo: Her True Story*. The swindles and trials of Soapy Smith and Lou Blonger in Denver are dealt with by prosecuting attorney Philip S. Van Dine in *Fighting the Underworld*. Harry Crawford can be found in Tom Gurr and H.H. Cox, *Famous Australian Crimes*. Horace Fuller examines the claims of some of the false dauphins in *Imposters and Adventurers*.

As for compilations, Ricky Jay's *Learned Pigs* and *Fireproof Women* and *Jay's Journal of Anomalies* are splendid as are Nick Yapp, *Hoaxers and their Victims*, Carl Sifakis, *Hoaxes & Scams* and Jay Robert Nash, *Hustlers & Conmen*. Racing frauds are dealt with entertainingly by David Ashforth in *Ringers & Rascals*.

Those who wish to read more of Princes Ubangi and her manager Joe Gardiner, Charles Wells, Horatio Bottomley, and Horatio Buckland will find their files at the National Archives, Kew. The file – which has a long account of his career – relating to the deportation of Von Veltheim is also at the Archives. Those interested in the insurance murders by Catherine Flanagan and Margaret Higgins might care to read Angela Brabin 'Arsenic and the Black Widows' in *History Today*, October 2002.

Index